THE WAY THINGS ARE

Other books in the Buddhism Today series
by Lama Ole Nydahl

Lama Ole Nydahl's works are translated into over a dozen
languages. For more information, please consult the Center
listed in your area.

The Way Things Are

*A Living Approach to Buddhism
for Today's World*

LAMA OLE NYDAHL

BLUE DOLPHIN
1996

Published by
Blue Dolphin Publishing, Inc.
P.O. Box 8, Nevada City, CA 95959
Orders: 1-800-643-0765

Firsr printing, September, 1996

Library of Congress Cataloging-in-Publication Data

Nydahl, Ole.
    The way things are : a living approach to Buddhism for
today's world / Ole Nydahl.
        p. cm.
    ISBN 0-931892-38-4
    1. Buddhism. I. Title.
BQ4012.N93 1996
294.3—dc20   96-35059
                                                           CIP

Printed in the United States of America by
Blue Dolphin Press, Grass Valley, California

5   4   3   2   1

Dedicated to my first teacher,
Lopon Chechoo Rinpoche

CONTENTS

*Head of the Karma Kagyu Lineage,
the 17th Karmapa, Thaye Dorje,
now in India*

Tibetan Buddhist Meditation

Buddhist Centre Edmonton Kamtsang Choling would like to invite anyone interested in learning more about Tibetan Buddhist meditation to join our weekly Three Lights meditation.

The Three Lights meditation is an example of a Guru Yoga (or meditation on the lama), one of the most powerful methods of Tibetan Buddhism. The meditation is guided and no preparation is required.

Buddhist Centre Edmonton was founded in the Karma Kagyu tradition by Lama Ole Nydahl, and operates under the spiritual guidance of H.H. Thaye Dorje, the 17th Gyalwa Karmapa.

We meet at 8:00 p.m. every Wednesday at 11643 - 111A Avenue. Please call Paul or Janice at 447-1845 for more details.

Karmapa Chenno

PREFACE

The recent opening of the West to Buddhism is no passing fad. As can be expected when teachings of such vastness are introduced, many fine translations and commentaries quickly appear. Missing until now, however, was a concise and practical overview of the whole subject. This book evolved during two decades of close work with thousands of students and focuses on daily life.

As no Buddhist needs to be politically correct, it includes a critical examination of world matters and points towards a maximum of human freedom and quality. Buddha's teachings come wonderfully alive when we put ourselves in his situation, and this book is my special thanks to the maturing lay teachers and yogis of the Karma Kagyu lineage around the world. It is printed in a dozen languages already and contains meditations which make concepts into experience.

I thank the many who helped to make it happen.

With blessings from the protectors, White Umbrella and Black Coat, *learn and enjoy!*

Tomek, Caty, Hannah, and Lama Ole

INTRODUCTION

Two thousand five hundred and fifty years ago, the historical Buddha enjoyed unique circumstances for passing on his teachings. Born into a highly developed culture, he was surrounded by exceedingly gifted people. After reaching enlightenment, he shared his methods for discovering the mind for a full forty-five years. It is for this reason that his teachings, called the Dharma, are so vast.

The *Kanjur*, Buddha's own words, consists of 108 volumes containing 84,000 helpful teachings. Later commentaries on these, the *Tenjur*, amount to another 254 equally thick books. This makes Buddha's final evaluation of his life understandable: "I can die happily. I did not hold one single teaching in a closed hand. Everything that may benefit you I have already given." His very last statement sets Buddhism apart from what is otherwise called religion: "Now, don't believe my words because a Buddha told you, but examine them well. Be a light onto yourselves."

Such statements show the practical approach of Buddhism which is meant for real life. When people asked Buddha why and what he taught, he replied: "I teach because you and all beings seek happiness and try to avoid suffering. I teach 'the way things are'."

Teachings of such vastness are best understood in the context of one's whole life. Their masterly structure becomes most evident when contrasted to a wide range of mental disciplines. Over the centuries, all attempts to contain the wealth of Buddhism within any conceptual framework have proven far too shallow. For example, many people today consider Buddhism to be a philosophy. This is true insofar as the teachings are completely logical. Stringency of thought is a natural result of Buddhist practice and arises from the experience of unimpeded inner space.

As clear thinking is surely central to a full development of mind, why then is Buddhism not a philosophy? Because the teachings change whoever gets involved with them. Philosophy explains things on the formal level of words and ideas, but when the books are re-shelved, not so much has happened.

Buddha's teachings, on the other hand, work with one's totality. They lead to permanent transformations because they give the key to inner and outer events experienced every day. Applying the teachings to one's life will develop a deep confidence in their skillfulness, and all life situations will have the added taste of meaning and growth.

A second group emphasizes the ability of the teachings to transform its practitioners and therefore considers Buddhism a kind of psychology. The aim of this noble trade is to improve people's lives. The varying schools of psychology all try to help people to neither burden society nor themselves during the sixty to eighty years that most stay around.

Buddhism, however, and especially The Diamond Way, becomes relevant at the point where people are mature and stable, where they experience space as blissful and not threatening. Until then, self-reliance is just a word. From this level of power the teachings develop courage, joy and love, which are mind's inherent wealth.

When one's awareness grows of the conditioned nature of all things, fixed concepts must fall away and the perfect qualities of body, speech and mind will begin to appear by themselves. It happens along these lines: as subject, object and action—the experiencer, the experienced, and the experience itself—become less separate, certain insights follow. The realization that there is no real or personal "self" will bring the ultimate security of liberation. This is the first step towards understanding the depth of the way and an unshakable basis for the full unfoldment of mind called enlightenment.

Both psychology and Buddhism have the capacity to change people, but Buddha's teaching is for the already healthy. Buddhism starts where psychology stops, and its aim is always full enlightenment—Buddhahood—the full-blown living state of perfection beyond concepts.

Again, some people maintain that Buddhism is a religion. It is true that practical benefits accrue from this status, such as a non-profit status, but the point is highly debatable. Buddhism certainly is not a "faith." One fundamental difference lies within the term "religion" itself. "Re-" in Latin means "again" and "ligare" means "to unite." Religion, therefore, tries to reunite beings or lead them back to something perfect.

Buddhism, on the contrary, seeks nothing in the past. If there was once a fall from a paradise, it would be unreliable and one might fall again! Truth, to be absolute, must be Truth at all times and places, which would automatically disprove any separate "outer" or "creating" entity. An examination of most gods which are worshipped around the world, whether possessive, jealous, or in the case of Allah, directly vengeful, makes it good common sense not to get involved with them. It is highly unwise to choose somebody for a god whom one would not like as a neighbor.

Buddha, on the other hand, is everybody's friend. He works only to free and enlighten beings and he has no other goal than their ultimate good. He wants colleagues, not followers, and burdens neither decency nor basic intelligence. In his teaching there are no religious death sentences as in Islam, no imposed guilt trips concerning sexuality, or church dogmas to merely believe. All Buddha's statements are logical, can be experienced, and liberate beings. They are also handy: to benefit from his teachings, one only needs confidence in a goal worth reaching—enlightenment (Buddha)—in the teachings (Dharma) taking one there and in one's friends (Sangha) on the way.

Neither is Buddhism "new age," where different spiritual traditions and "soft" sciences are mixed to fit the wishes of those who would rather feel good than question things. Though it is impressive that the humanism of the idealistic sixties could survive into the chrome-plated world of the "me" generation, such conditioned "truths" can be trusted even less than paradises which may again be lost. Whether outer or inner, whatever appears at a certain time and place must have arisen from conditions. This being so, it will change and disappear again. Also, on the level of visible symbols: although crystals are central to the "new age," and the highest level of Buddha's teachings is called the Diamond Way: the latter is *not* the snob or upscale edition of the former.

What then, does Buddha teach? He affirms an all-pervading, timeless truth, containing and knowing everything, both relative and absolute. Being inseparable from space it may be experienced as one's own mind under given circumstances. This state is called the level of truth and nothing is ever separate from it. Experiencing its nature as spontaneous joy and expressing active compassion, it is the source of every perfection.

It is unique that Buddha relies on the maturity of his students and that he sees no need to control them with punishing or judging gods. Instead, he gives practical advice and shows the world to be a collective dream, originating from the basic consciousness of all beings. Inside this common frame, the imprints of their actions— also called "karmas"—mature from life to life. These karmas bring about rebirths with varying bodies and abilities in the very different countries of the world, and are the cause of all conditioned experience.

So, what is Buddhism? Buddha used the best description himself. During the 1,500 years the teachings existed in India, they were called Dharma, and for the last 1,000 years in Tibet, the name was Chö. Both mean "the way things are." Understanding "the way things are" is the key to every happiness. Buddha himself is both teacher, example, protector and friend. His help allows beings to avoid suffering and to enter a state of increasing bliss while also liberating and enlightening others.

THE WAY THINGS ARE

BUDDHA'S LIFE

BIRTH AND YOUTH AT COURT

An overview of Buddha's life brings his teachings much closer. He was born into a royal family 2,580 years ago and probably looked European: the texts describe him as tall, strong, and blue-eyed. His parents' kingdom lay at the southern border of today's Nepal around the town then called Kapilavastu. Excavations show it to have possessed both a sewage system and central heating, luxurious compared to the present Lumbini nearby and to many third world towns today.

The boy was decidedly no virgin birth, but was the very last opportunity for his mother to have a child, and shortly after he was born, three yogis told his parents this: "He is truly special. If he is not confronted with the suffering of the world, he will become everything you wish him to be. A strong king, he will conquer the neighboring kingdoms and fulfill all your expectations. If, however, he perceives the suffering inherent in conditioned existence, he will renounce his position and bring enlightening insights into the world."

His parents wanted an heir to their kingdom and no poet, dreamer or philosopher, so they decided to be very careful. They surrounded the young prince with everything a healthy young man likes: beautiful women—the texts say 500 of them—opportunities for sports and excitement, and the finest teachers for his education. Whatever he wished for, he just

needed to point. Also, his subconscious contained no disturbing impressions which might surface, so up until the age of
twenty-nine, he knew only joy. Then, however, his world
turned upside down.

DISAPPOINTMENT AND SEARCH FOR TRUTH

Since the yogis' prediction, everything unpleasant had
been kept away from the future Buddha. Therefore he
witnessed suffering only late in his life, but then in its main
physical expressions. On three consecutive days, he saw
somebody very sick, someone old, and someone dead. His
recognition that sickness, old age, and death are part of every
life shook him to his roots and, after returning to his palace,
he had a bad night. Wherever he searched, he found nothing
on which his friends and he could truly rely. Fame, pleasure,
and possessions would all disappear. Whether he looked
outside or inside, everything was impermanent. There was
nothing lasting anywhere.

The next morning he passed a Yogi in deep meditation,
and their minds met. The future Buddha knew that he had
found a true refuge. This man seemed to experience something real and timeless. He was conscious not only of his own
thoughts and feelings and the various conditions outside, but
of his own awareness. The yogi's state of mind awakened the
prince to everyone's true essence: the all-knowing space
which makes everything possible; its radiant clarity which
playfully expresses mind's richness as inner and outer mani-
festation, and its limitless love that obstructs nothing. So that
was it! In a flash the prince realized that the absolute truth he
had been searching for was nothing but mind itself.

At his time, there were no spiritual "turbo chargers" or "fast
lanes" such as contained in the Tibetan teachings of Maha-

mudra or Maha Ati, the Chag Chen or Dzog Chen. These most efficient of methods Buddha could only show *after* his enlightenment. Nobody in his time possessed a "view" of life which integrated all aspects of life into the path, like brushing your teeth, making love, thinking, sleeping or eating, and used them to recognize one's mind. As "riding the great tiger of immediate experience" was not possible then, the prince could only choose the much slower path of renouncing the world. He had to limit the number of daily distractions. Cutting off a most enjoyable private life, he disappeared into the hills and woods of northern India.

Wanting beyond all things to realize the nature of mind, there was no time for a leisurely search, and his next six years were hard. While he stayed in the woods and clearings of northern India, the young prince perfected even the most extreme practices given to him. And, as his motivation sometimes outran his judgment, he once nearly starved himself to death. He learned from the finest teachers available at his time and practiced within all the schools of thought known also today. Spanning the areas of materialism, nihilism, transcendentalism and existentialism he quickly outpaced his successive gurus, but each time found himself no closer to his goal. However well they might control the events taking place in mind, nobody knew mind itself. At the end of each path there was nothing permanent in which he could build his trust.

CONDITIONS IN ANCIENT NORTHERN INDIA

An unusual spiritual openness enriched the India of Buddha's times—comparable to that of ancient Greece, the Renaissance and our own "sixties." Even though the most recent surge left a lot of casualties due to drugs, such frontal attacks on materialism and authority are noble and of utmost importance. People in the sixties were idealistic and strove, though often short-sightedly, for the happiness of all. Blind to emerging ghettos, overpopulation and other looming dangers to the world, they expressed their idealism on many levels, trusted in the basic goodness of beings, and avoided becoming snobs. Possibly due to the lack of birth-control, the atmosphere surrounding Buddha seems to have been more prudish than today, but concerning the clarity of mind, many of his students must have been a joy to teach. The above mentioned philosophies were already known then, and many Indians of that time actually expected spirituality to influence their lives positively.

Whenever dualistic philosophies are allowed to pervade every aspect of existence, freedom suffers badly! Where it happened and people allowed a power structure to disseminate it, the result was burned witches, Communism, Nazism, quotas or political correctness. A non-dualistic teaching like Buddhism, however, is intrinsically harmless. Also, where Buddhism is the dominant religion, it contains no danger to freedom. It teaches a variety of methods from which different beings can freely choose, avoids applying pressure through society, and never motivates through fear.

Where Buddhism arose, not only were safeguards against abuse of spiritual power expected, but the teachings themselves were also severely tested. Any view introduced was open to harsh and critical debate. It must transcend personal wishes and point to a permanent truth. If there was no proper *view,* no defined *methods* to be practiced, and no *goal* that could be verified, it did not qualify. Teachers were then very careful about bringing forth half-baked insights. Spiritual honesty demanded that whoever lost one of the frequent philosophical debates automatically became the winner's student.

BUDDHA'S ENLIGHTENMENT

After six anonymous years in the then still agreeable northern India, the young prince came to what is now called Bodhgaya. (Today it is a village full of local beggars and foreign temples situated two-thirds of the way from Delhi to Calcutta in the utterly overpopulated state of Bihar.) Upon arrival, this deep motivation to benefit beings awakened, and settling under a vast tree near a small river, he decided to meditate there and fully develop his mind. One week later, on the full moon of May, he reached his goal. The day he became a Buddha was his thirty-fifth birthday, and forty-five years later he died on that same full moon.

As enlightenment dissolved the last veils that covered his mind, the perceived separation between space and energy in and around him disappeared, and he became timeless, all-knowing awareness. Various traditions explain the process differently, but in the highest view, that of the Maha Anuttara Yoga Tantra, the all-pervading truth-nature manifesting as the Buddhas of past, present and future blessed him. They condensed their perfect wisdom into the form of Sarva Buddha Dakini, a white female Buddha, and through her union with him, their male and female energies merged into perfection as did all other dualities.

Through every atom of his body he *knew* everything and was *all*. Crossing the river from the place where he had reached his goal, the Buddha stayed for three weeks below the now famous tree at Bodhgaya. Then he gave refuge[1] to several gods and trained his body to handle the intense flow of enlightened energies, but taught no human beings there.

His first teaching for humans was given four weeks later at the Deer Park near Sarnath, a village about halfway between Delhi and Calcutta. The neighboring town of Benares is very holy to the Hindus. They burn their dead at the banks of the

Ganges and throw the remains into the river. A complete pilgrimage to the site includes such delicacies as bathing in the vast stream and drinking its water.

The five truth seekers who first came to him were not the most attractive of students. Being grumpy by nature, they had adored him while he practiced extreme austerities but were now disgusted at his radiant joy and health. Understanding such states to be "worldly" and thinking mainly of themselves, they were the very clients to quickly send somewhere else. When curiosity got the better of their fixed ideas, however, they could only ask: "Why do you shine like that? What happened to you?" His answer to them was the famous "Four Noble Truths" which today have slightly different wordings in various traditions. Buddha must have expressed them somewhat like this: Conditioned existence is suffering. Suffering has a cause. It has an end and there are ways leading to that end.

BUDDHA'S TEACHING
IN ITS TOTALITY

THE SMALL WAY—THERAVADA
(THE FOUR NOBLE TRUTHS)

During the forty-five years following the Buddha's enlightenment, the Four Noble Truths supplied a frame for his teachings and were explained according to the intelligence of his listeners. Though worded to mainly attract self-centered people, these Truths continue to influence all Buddhist schools. Because the questioning minds of the West are today the natural beneficiaries and future of Buddhism, it does not matter that our present interpretations widely transcend the horizons of the people to whom the teachings were originally given.

Already Buddha's first words: "There is suffering," need much elucidation. When meeting that quote for the first time, many consider it basically depressing. Compared to the self-representations of belief-religions which claim their gods to be the only, or strongest, or Allah's revenge to be "merciless and unfailing," it does not give weak people the feeling of being part of a big thing. Instead, one has to think a bit, but if one does, Buddha's first words point toward limitless happiness. And how?

What nearly everyone forgets is the conditioned nature of their experiences, that these depend on the level from which they are made. Twenty years as a lama have shown me that people are very aware of their changing feelings, always believing what is on their inner screen now to be real. This tendency is independent of their intelligence. People certainly do not need a Buddha to tell them that there exist happy and unhappy days. What everybody needs the Buddha for is what one does *not* know or readily see: without him one misses the mirror behind the pictures, the unconditioned state of awareness, the highest joy which is inseparable from the full functioning of mind.

"There is suffering" thus encompasses all non-enlightened existence. In comparison to the continuous freshness of mind's timeless play, everything else appears simply shallow. To the knower of the radiance of limitless space, even the finest conditioned experiences are less; the most beautiful wave is less fulfilling than the ocean itself.

This is why the first of Buddha's Four Noble Truths is not pessimistic, as might appear at first glance, but actually very uplifting. Whoever shows the nature of indestructible mind to be more perfect than anything we have ever experienced, makes us boundlessly rich.

Buddha's second statement: "Suffering has a cause," also calls for some intelligent evaluation. What could be a plausible reason for everything—from sharpest pain to slight boredom or frustration? Clearly not the absolutely evil principles or "devils" of dualistic belief-religions. The law of action and reaction functions endlessly, and something absolutely evil is forced to self-destruct. What concerns suffering, Buddha knows only one culprit: the basic ignorance of unenlightened mind. Functioning like an eye, the unenlightened mind experiences events outer and inner, but not itself. This inability to recognize the seer, the thing seen, and the act of seeing as conditioning one another and as parts of the same totality is its ignorance. Everyone can check out for themselves how many passing objects, situations, and states of mind one can be aware of, and even take very seriously, while one totally misses and has no idea of the timeless essence experiencing it all. This very inability of unenlightened mind to recognize itself is the cause of the conditioned world and the reason for all suffering.

Due to mind's only partial functioning, the illusion of separation and the dualistic view arise. Though there is nothing permanent or lasting, either inside or outside, the space-like nature of mind—the seer—feels itself to be an "I," and what appears in that space becomes a "you," or "something separate." Although everything conditioned changes constantly and has no actual existence, the force of habit and the coarseness of sense-impressions make unenlightened beings believe that appearances are real.

The separation between an "I" and a "you," a "here" and a "there," causes disturbing feelings to arise: attachment to what one wants, and ill-will against what is deemed unpleasant. Attachment then brings greed: what one likes, one wants to keep; and aversion becomes envy: those one dislikes, one does not want to see happy. Basic ignorance itself, the cause of all the difficulties, produces the exclusive, and harmful, kind of pride. Here, momentary conditions such as friends, wealth, or beauty, situations where one might excel, are believed to be real, and one does not recognize one's inability to control or even keep them. The *inclusive* pride, on the other hand, should be a yogi's constant state. Seeing the power, potential, and truth nature of all beings and in every situation, one is already in a pure land and will both learn from and spontaneously benefit others.

The above-mentioned six disturbing emotions, all arising from ignorance, may manifest in 84,000 combinations, and although they change constantly, one still holds them to be real. During the present moment of an experience, non-meditators cannot recognize that these emotions were not there before, are changing right now, and will not be there later; and that it is actually stupid to give them energy. Instead, people involve their body, speech and mind with such passing states and thus continuously sow seeds of future suffering, both in their subconscious and in the world. When these later mature as further difficulties, few will not seek the fault with others. Forgetting that oneself is the sole cause for what happens, one will blame society, family, partners or whatever else is in vogue. Rather than use the precious opportunity to understand and change habits from former lives and this one, one will again plant the seeds of future tightness and pain.

Buddha's third Noble Truth, at this historic encounter 2,550 years ago, deeply moves the West today. Fearlessly he presented himself as having reached the "goal." With the full power of his authority he proclaimed the "end to suffering," the state of total perfection which he now ceaselessly experienced himself. For the first time in history, here was something "absolute" that beings could strive for, a real refuge for all. Whoever has meditated with the right instructions since that time has confirmed parts or all of his highest insight. When one recognizes ultimate truth as being in its essence fearless all-knowing space, in its experience highest continuous joy, and in its expression active compassion—beyond the concept of anybody doing something to anyone—everything becomes meaning and joy. In enlightenment, mind is like the sun. It radiates on all and through its own power.

In Sarnath, where still today a vast Stupa in ruins celebrates the event, Buddha's fourth Noble Truth set the direction for his own activity and the lives of countless fine teachers until now. Stating: "There is a way to the ending of suffering" he began forty-five years of incessant work to set beings free. Frequently surrounded by highly exciting and intelligent people, he could thus share the 84,000 teachings which are now becoming accessible to our world.

As the first group of Buddha's students were small-minded, and only interested in their own welfare, they would hardly have accepted the following explanations as the inner meaning of his words to them. For that reason his teachings on mind's unfoldment through three levels and five wisdoms were included in his "Great Way" of compassionate action for others.

His highest teaching, called the "Diamond Way," involves the transformation of body, speech and mind. It moves on from the level of concepts and ideas to a complete identification with enlightenment and spontaneous activity. It focuses on the four kinds of liberating activities springing from enlightened insight and confirms fearlessness, spontaneous joy and active compassion as being one's true nature. Central views are of course shared by all Buddhists everywhere, and all agree that the difference between a Buddha and everyone else is that Buddha fulfilled the conditions for enlightenment. Unenlightened beings still have to do that work.

THE GREAT WAY—MAHAYANA
(COMPASSION AND WISDOM)

Eight years after his first teaching at Sarnath, people of a totally different kind came to learn from Buddha at Rajgir, a mountain some hours north of Bodhgaya. They had energy for others and enjoyed a broad, robust view of life. Working with this surplus of good will, Buddha showed how loving compassion may be strengthened until any separation experienced between subject, object and action falls away.

At the same time, he gave his students the tools for realizing their natural wisdom. He taught them to see what really is, uncolored by concepts, attachment, or fear. Above all, he insisted that compassion and wisdom grow in balance. With only the first, one becomes dogmatic and sentimental,

while insight alone makes one cold and unmotivated. Beings
need both.

Compassion

At the first stage of compassion, one likes other beings
when they behave according to one's expectations. Many
have surely accomplished this: it satisfies one's sense of order.

The second level begins when one wishes others good,
even when they are difficult. One understands that the cause
of harmful actions is basic ignorance. All beings want happiness, but if one does not know what brings this about, one's
mistakes will continue to cause suffering for others and
oneself. Lacking awareness of cause and effect, many grab the
nettles and miss the flowers.

The perfection of compassion is truly vast. It is like the sun
which shines on everyone. On this level one does not
discriminate, but simply does one's best while one's surroundings receive blessing, purification, or teachings according to their karma and intelligence. This non-discriminating
compassion goes beyond any like or dislike and matures
beings in the quickest possible way.

The first two steps are like projecting beautiful pictures on
the screen of one's mind. The third, however, is the radiance
of mind itself. At first one keeps losing the experience, but
once stabilized, its power only grows.

Wisdom

There are two kinds of wisdom. The worldly kind relates
to all outer and inner phenomena experienced by mind, while
liberating wisdom points to mind itself.

The first wisdom is taught in schools and universities. It enables one to make more money in a shorter time, do more interesting work, and die with a larger debt than one's uneducated neighbor. This kind of wisdom is limited to what is impermanent, and at one's grave, its benefits are gone. While one may expect that developing one's intelligence in this life may lead one to choose bright future parents, then as a known Danish proverb states, "The last shirt has no pockets."

Wisdom of mind itself, however, liberates and enlightens and can never be lost. Being unlimited clear space, awareness was never born and also cannot die; its qualities are unconditioned and lasting. From lifetime to lifetime, the polished parts of the mind's mirror—the realized aspects of awareness—will remain or be easily rediscovered. From the level where compassion has arisen, however, and one no longer takes experiences personally, but as expressions of cause and effect, personal realizations can only increase until complete enlightenment.

So, how does mind recognize itself? By introducing ever more words and concepts? Do the monks of the "virtuous" or Gelugpa School of Tibetan Buddhism, who dissect philosophical points for days with the finest of intellectual tools, manifest many enlightenments? On the contrary, *not* minding thoughts is the way to go. The key point here is being spontaneous and effortless. By leaving the experiencer to rest in its own space while staying naturally with what is, mind becomes calm and its radiant essence automatically manifests.

The goal is none other than mind's natural state. In this way, first liberating and then enlightening wisdoms arise, and the world is recognized as the dream—both collective as well as individual—which it is. Acting from the realization that subject, object, and action are interdependent, one does whatever brings growth, meaning, and joy.

Unenlightened beings miss their innate perfection because of basic ignorance. Depending on one's wishes, this
state may be understood as consisting of either four or two
veils. In the former case, one distinguishes between basic
ignorance, the disturbing feelings arising from it, the clumsy
actions which follow, and the unpleasant results and short-
sighted habits which propel one into further harm. This was
the explanation Buddha chose for his second Noble Truth.

According to the second view, constantly changing states
of mind are one's first obstacle. Whoever goes up and down
between conditioned states of happiness and suffering, observing the world through the rosy or black glasses of likes
and dislikes, will not see what is really there. The second
hindrance is stiff ideas and the narrowing of experience
through concepts—materialistic, nihilistic, existential, tran-
scendental or whatever. The finger pointing to the moon is
not the moon, and words and ideas are only the shadow of
experience. Whichever of the two definitions one chooses—
and the precious cake of Buddha's teaching can be cut in
many other interesting ways—when everything limiting is
removed, mind realizes its true nature.

As passing emotions such as ignorance, anger, jealousy,
pride and attachment are considered "real" and are taken so
seriously by those they afflict, here is some advice on how to
weaken and even transform them.

The Disturbing Emotions—
as Sources of the Five "Female" Wisdoms

While an expanding mind will naturally seek the more
exciting spontaneity of the Diamond Way, the union of space
and joy, it is both necessary and wise to emphasize its
motivation and philosophy, the Great Way of compassion and
wisdom. The idea of transforming and not suppressing the

difficult states of mind—which are traditionally targeted with little humor as "sinful" or "antisocial" by various religions and political groups—is like coming up for air. With this realization, moral tightness quickly dissolves and everything is open and can be worked with. Handled intelligently, disturbing feelings become the raw material for enlightenment and connect beings with the highest realizations of the five Buddha families, the expressions of complete enlightenment.

Though less effective than the Diamond Way, where one behaves like a Buddha until becoming one, a growing intellectual understanding of the conditioned nature of everything outer and inner, and a strong wish for the benefit of others, will in time transform any emotional energy into mind's above-mentioned five inherent wisdoms. Described as mirrorlike, equalizing, discriminating, all-performing, and intuitive or all-pervading, they are inseparable from awareness itself.

Buddha thus advises a concerted three-step attack on this imaginary but tough enemy. First, one should avoid circumstances known to bring about unwanted feelings. If that is not possible, one is wise to focus on their impermanent condition and changing nature: as a certain disturbing mental state was not present earlier and will soon be gone again, it would be nonsense to act it out, thus laying the seeds for future trouble.

The highest level is not giving power to unwanted feelings by "letting the thief come to an empty house." Here, one stays strictly with what is in front of one's nose and neither acknowledges nor identifies with any disturbance. As this succeeds, one realizes, ever more consciously and with growing amazement and joy, that painful mind-states do not just vanish into nothingness but actually reappear in their pure form, as five liberating wisdoms. The way dirt becomes compost or molten iron is turned into useful objects, disturbing feelings transform into insights beyond ego.

Though superficial variations may exist, Buddha's enlightened view and the experiences of Buddhist yogis over the last
twenty-five centuries agree on the input-output of this transformation: when *anger* returns to the mind, one will see
everything *clearly as in a mirror,* and the state is symbolized
by a diamond; nothing is added nor withdrawn. "Exclusive"
pride which makes one stiff and unable to share, will become
an experience of *the richness of existence,* often compared to
many jewels. *Attachment* will change into *discriminating
wisdom,* the ability to understand phenomena both as they are
in themselves and as parts of a totality; warm and all-
embracing, it is likened to a lotus-flower. *Jealousy,* skillfully
feeding on both something and nothing, will transform into a
swordlike power to cut through. It is a state of continuous
experience called *all-performing wisdom.* Even mind's most
persistent veil, *confusion* and *stupidity,* will dissolve when
short bursts of intense awareness are developed on the basis
of right methods and deep confidence. They will then turn
into an *intuitive wisdom* which contains everything everywhere. It is all-knowing because space and energy is the same
at all times and places. Enlightened mind is seen to not be
separate from anything.

Taking Buddhist refuge plants indestructible seeds for
liberation and later enlightenment but does not mean the
immediate end to all unwanted states of mind. Therefore, until
one's practice of the beyond-conceptual Diamond Way
makes everything spontaneously pure, here is some advice
for home, work and love during the period one is still caught
inside the realm of thought and conditioned feelings.

With upcoming anger, be totally aware. If there is immediate danger, quickly remove its cause, but in case of a
psychological nuisance, simply observe the unpleasant situation and let it pass. Don't act or speak on a burst of aggression,
but be the big dog who does not need to bark; he is strong
enough. Harmful people are more confused than evil and,

while a few minutes in their company is trying to others, they have to live with themselves day and night. Hurting them in addition to such suffering would be unsportsmanlike. Instead, it is wise to give any difficult situation lots of space, learn from it for the later benefit of all, and then quickly let it go. If that is not possible, especially women may seek relief by talking about their troubles. One should not make this a habit, however. It is a major cause of loneliness.

If one is struck with the exclusive kind of pride, the awareness of everybody's Buddha nature is an effective antidote. People are also helped by realizing that Heaven and Hell happen between their ears, ribs or wherever else they assume their mind to be; that their experience of the outer world depends on their inner condition and that highest truth is always highest joy. Seeing beings as attractive and meaningful brings only good, while searching for their faults produces spiritual poverty. It is simply difficult to unfold one's potential in bad company. We ourselves decide if the cup is half full or half empty!

Within the vast field of attachments, the special realm of humans, hopefully good karmic bonds from former lives will allow one to share at least one's sexual desires for the pleasure also of one's partners. Whatever happiness is not attainable for oneself here and now, one should always wish for others, while not forgetting the impermanence of every conditioned state. Only enlightenment means ultimate and lasting happiness, and it matters little whether one will reach one's grave in a Mazda or a Mercedes.

Jealousy is an especially tenacious enemy. It can sustain itself on anything or nothing and may influence mind for a long time. Therefore envy is an excellent guinea pig for examining one's consciousness, showing clearly how well mind handles its projections. For this feeling, I know only one cure, but it liberates right away: one should wish the object of jealousy so much of what one desires for oneself that these feelings transcend all concepts and enter the world of fairy tales. Wish them the best job, a car so long they can hardly park it, a hundred healthy lovers every night, and enough time for enjoying it all!

The difficulty in transforming stupidity is that some will never understand quantum physics nor the intellectual teachings on the sixteen levels of emptiness.[2] The latter point, which in Buddhism is also called voidness and no-thing-ness, means that nothing exists in itself but arises from conditions. It describes the ultimate nature of everything outer and inner, and though it is spontaneously realized in flashes of insight between thoughts—often in unusual situations—comprehending it through concepts is slow and involves major brain-gymnastics. Luckily in this quest it is possible to use all parts of the mind together. Integrated through the total experience of meditation, an intellectual analysis of phenomena may explain, feed on, and even enrich one's daily life. If one makes no problem of a less agile mind, practices to capacity, and follows one's best understanding, qualities like compassion, confidence, and courage will make up for a moderate IQ.

Using Buddha's advice to transcend attachment and aversion in one's meditation, without forced intellectualization, intuitive insight must arise. Focusing strongly when possible and then relaxing, mind—like a cup of coffee—will reflect things once it has become still. The hooks of Buddha's enlightened teachings will catch the rings of mind's inherent wisdom, and the students will discover their true qualities in the fearless space of the lama's mind. The all-pervading wisdom thus realized is also called intuition. One knows things because of being one with them, and discovers space to be nothing separating or dead, but a container which conveys everything.

THE DIAMOND WAY—VAJRAYANA (HIGHEST VIEW)

The Diamond Way is the crown jewel of the Buddha's teaching. Working from the level of consequence and inspired insight to transform all experience into self-liberating meaning and natural purity, it employs methods of total identification with enlightenment for quickest results.

Both the Four Noble Truths on causality, and the inner or "Mahayana" teaching of the Buddha on compassion and wisdom, were given at fixed places. He taught them at Sarnath and Rajgir, respectively, in northeast India. Concerning the Diamond Way, this is only partially so. Though the more theoretical instructions on the Buddha-nature of all beings were given at Shravasti and Vaishali, wherever exciting and creative people full of life and joy came to him, Buddha taught spontaneously and through immediate experience. There were amazing meetings where he connected beings with their timeless clear light, and, driven by their affinity for enlightenment and unable to experience Buddha as "outside" or separate from themselves, the strong devotion of these students made them absorb his qualities quickly. By recognizing the Mahamudra which the Buddha taught as their own essence, and the energy fields of the Buddha-aspects as their own enlightened qualities, they were able to free the richness which had grown in them over lifetimes.

The feeling of devotion, though so useful when the teacher is mature and responsible, has many sides and can lead to very different results. Khomeini, Pol Pot, Hitler and Stalin were visibly bad. They could, however, still destroy massive amounts of happiness and life because stupid and trusting people believed in them. On the other hand, devotion to the Buddha and other compassionate teachers who transparently do as they say has helped many tremendously. As sincere devotion has the power to take beings beyond duality, over centuries it has brought many to liberation and enlightenment, or at least helped them to lead meaningful and conscious lives.

With such different outcomes from the same feeling, it is wise to examine its nature. As devotion springs from a sense of identification, its object is essential. Of course it is a strong experience to meet the outer expression of one's deep feeling or conviction, but when the rush is over, who wants to be left with a catastrophic hangover? That is why it is so important which example one will identify with. A Khomeini evidently reflects one's cold hate, and a Shoko Ashahara one's potential for scheming, whereas a Buddha manifests mind's timeless luminosity and compassion. Today it is up to people's critical education and an inquisitive—but fair—press to make the useful examples attractive and expose the bad ones till nobody will go near.

The Four Buddha-Activities, Mind's "Male" Expression.

The Diamond Way is the field of spontaneously being in the world and brings forth one's beyond-personal Buddha-activities in the fastest way. The methods employed integrate beings' increasingly perfect actions as they push their way through the layers of habitual behavior and become a total enlightened expression. Utilizing their potential means benefiting countless beings.

From the ultimate view of these highest teachings, masculine "joy" is expressed by the diamond, in essence indestructible and naturally radiant. Springing spontaneously from the fearless compassion of space, calming, increasing, fascinating and powerfully protective qualities manifest whenever needed and where a connection to enlightenment exists. To give a taste of their breadth and width, these enlightened activities are listed below under slightly different headings.

Peace-giving: If students are fragile like broken eggs or hard like marble ones, "being kind" is often the right approach. In the first case, they receive a healing dose of confidence in their potential, and in the second, the lack of outside pressure forces them out of their shells and they must communicate. Conditions must not long stay sweet and warm, however. When basic trust has arisen and before habits and laziness can set in, people should be made to learn

Enriching: When inner peace has liberated the necessary energy, the teacher's job is to introduce the possibilities which life offers. Such growth should be entered upon gradually, however. If people overestimate their newly-found security, try too many things at the same time and then fall on their noses, their illusory ego has an excuse for again tightening its hold. Therefore: to increasingly experience things as rich and beautiful, it is wise to start small and finish things step by step.

So far the lama mainly needs to examine his students. Do they become self-reliant, develop a healthy sense of humor towards sex and life, and display an increasing surplus of good energy and actions for others? Do both he and they agree that life is becoming more meaningful?

Watching only one's students is not sufficient on the level of the two next activities. As they invoke more emotion and involve a closer exchange, it is vitally important that the teacher knows himself and his motivation, and is in full control. As unbroken confidence is so essential for the mental health of the student who should have every means for checking the teacher, this is the place for also mentioning some instances where a religious guiding role was abused.

Sharing fascination: If one has the power to influence others, growth can happen very quickly, as beings may readily identify with one's qualities. However, one may also cause much harm. Recent religion-based scandals in and around the civilized world have included mass suicides in the

Americas by Christian sects and devoutly Catholic tribes chopping up a million of their own kind in Africa. Several Hindu gurus have become very rich or erratic, and a yoga-teacher had poison-gas sprayed in a Japanese subway. Probably nobody informed expects anything but hate and suppression from Islam, but also several Rinpoches, organizations, and monks manage to produce hefty embarrassments in Buddha's good name. The goal of Buddha's teachings is always mind's full development and not the commandments of some dogmatic god. It is a fact which should facilitate intelligent behavior, but living up to an acceptable level of integrity still does not seem easy to many. All teachers share a vast responsibility here because any abuse in the field of teacher-students is poison to the increasing number of bright people who choose Buddhism to make quality out of their lives.

Actually in Buddhism there is no need to put on an artificial face or pretend anything. A Lama's freedom of action is vast, and whether one is celibate, lay or yogi, safeguarding one's students basically means being honest. If one works hard, knows the teachings well and says and does the same thing, it is their choice if they want the qualities which the teacher so openly displays. Such transparency is necessary for the lasting growth of any spiritual system based on a free choice, and hopefully it will be easier to maintain for the new generations of lay, Western teachers than it was for many of the traditional Asian lamas from whom we take over. It seems a major handicap to one's trust in others to come from one of the cultures where one is beaten frequently as a child!

So, to balance the things better not done: what should lamas keep in mind to be of real benefit? That one's only job is to make one's students independent, compassionate, and strong. To always celebrate their qualities and be thankful that it is possible to share so much good. To encourage them to understand the workings of the world and express themselves without any restraints by political correctness or other holy cows. One may share love, excitement, and whatever else benefits both students and teacher, but must never make them small. Knowing more, one is responsible for the student's development as long as they keep the bond, and should impart one's life-experience and set them on useful paths of growth.

On the highest level, the lama lets the students enter the fearless mirror-cabinet of his mind. When they discover that they are of that same nature, nothing more remains to be found. Duping newcomers with cultural mannerisms, alien dresses, or other props they have no chance to evaluate or understand should of course be avoided and will later backfire, while meeting people straight on brings lasting friendships. To sum it up: the teacher does right in avoiding any kind of pride when sharing fascination or guiding others to strong experiences.

Powerfully protecting: The fourth activity also calls for hard self-scrutiny on the side of the teacher: destroying and controlling activity must happen without anger. Only those who see the inherent Buddha-nature of others can treat them "roughly" without making mistakes and only those who are fearless themselves can use this important tool without ultimately getting into trouble. Though a "soft" spiritual atmosphere is preferred by nearly everybody, in a rough and tumble world, avoiding issues offers no protection and will not work. Most people would rather not discriminate or be critical, and this makes their spirituality vulnerable and confused. Much money and power chases spirituality, while the traditional checks on the teacher are frequently forgotten when they move to foreign cultures. Also, many untrained people want a slice of this easy new market and aim for recognition by saying whatever is "in," "progressive," or politically correct at the time, thus misguiding their students. Only those lamas who face difficult and embarrassing situations squarely and risk their popularity by cutting through confusion are really mature and responsible, and only their work will bring lasting results.

Though vows from former lives may produce the natural inclination to protect others: until disturbing ill-will can be sidelined or transformed, the teacher still has to observe that any forceful act be without self-motivation. A good doctor operates only to avoid later pain.

Potential of the Diamond Way

To whom, then, was this third level of teachings given? When students saw the Buddha as no god, person, or outer force, but trusted him as the mirror of their own mind, Buddha taught the Diamond Way and the Mahamudra. Awakening their qualities through his power and insight, he employed countless skillful means to fully develop them. In essence this ultimate or "third" level consists of three approaches: one of "devotion," one of "methods," and one of "insight," and mind recognizes itself either through its power of identification, its energy, or awareness.

If one's teacher is dependable, the most practiced meditation in the West today, Guru Yoga, contains the broadest contact to enlightenment. A specialty of the Karma Kagyu lineage, it is called "Lami Naljor" in Tibetan and "Guru Yoga" in Sanskrit, and also includes the ways of method and insight. Though it was less available in Tibet, Guru Yoga is the quickest shortcut to enlightenment for those who can use it. By permitting the use of even the most everyday situations to recognize the perfect nature of the here and now, it activates all qualities of the student. Wherever a degree of devotion is present, Guru Yoga is a meaningful first try. Its foundation is the rare confidence that things are in essence pure, and that one does not need to die to go to a Pure Land nor go elsewhere to see Buddhas, and that all one needs to do is to remove one's veils; however, not everybody finds this way suitable.

The preservation of these means of transformation is due to unbroken lineages of great yogis. Prominent among them is the hero Marpa, the father of the Kagyu lineage in Tibet. About 950 years ago, he traveled south to India three times, gathering and realizing the most important transmissions. During the Muslim destruction of the then high culture of Northern India, he brought the essential teachings back over the Himalayas to Tibet, where later the Karmapa incarnates united them with what was left of the earlier transmission through Guru Rinpoche. As this is clearly the main area of interest to the educated world today, here is some additional information on how the three approaches work.

With his way of power or "methods," Buddha awakened the qualities inherent in beings' energy systems. By emanating out the single male or female Buddha aspects, or transforming his own body into the united light forms known to many from Tibetan exhibitions or art books, he gave his students access to real enlightened feedback. According to their wishes and abilities, they could now meditate on peaceful or protective manifestations of mind's full unfoldment suitable to their own characteristics and thus bring about the wished-for beyond-personal changes.

The corresponding mantras[3] linked their vibration to those of the Buddha-aspects, also bringing liberating qualities to their speech and, during the phase of melting together with the Buddhas and staying in that awareness without center or circumference, effortless clarity entered their lives. The recognition that space and joy are inseparable must then develop into the lasting experience of Mahamudra, everywhere and in all situations.

The same goal is obtained through the way of insight. Necessitating neither month-long retreats nor extreme physical conditions like the above teachings, it is handier for the modern world but also takes longer. After mind has been calmed and held by staying with one's breath, an ordinary outer object or a Buddha form, intuition and penetrating insight, will appear and naturally grow. The continuation also of the space-awareness obtained on the "way of insight" are the four levels of Mahamudra.

Mind is best recognized in daily life through identification with a compassionate Lama who is beyond fear. If one can rest in such a teacher's mind-space till one develops all one's inherent qualities, there will be amazing growth. When Buddha shared his enlightenment as the Mahamudra and the Diamond Way, it happened so directly that there was no room for doubt. Both in their practical exchange and through his highest teachings on view and formal initiations, he imparted to his students the unlimited experience of subject, object and action being interdependent and basically one. From then till today, this transmission has freed countless beings. Mental processes become relaxed and effortless, happiness has no alternative, and people feel at home in any situation. After an introduction to such timeless wisdom, mind's self-liberating processes awaken and remove all obstructions till the goal is reached.

The Ways of "Methods," of "Insight" and of "Guru Yoga"

Over the years, a conceptual approach to Buddhism has also developed. Gifted students became professors of Tibetan and Buddhology and there now exists the important KIBI university in Delhi, a bridge of learning to the world. The

The Ways of "Methods," of "Insight," and of "Guru Yoga"

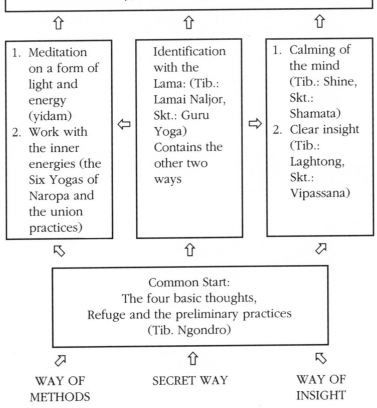

The Common Goal:
Enlightenment: Highest Realization and non-dual awareness through the one or four steps of the **Mahamudra**: "Rainbow-body" or the way through "One-Pointedness," "Non-Artificiality," "One Taste," and "Non-Meditation"

⇧ ⇧ ⇧

1. Meditation on a form of light and energy (yidam)
2. Work with the inner energies (the Six Yogas of Naropa and the union practices)

⇦

Identification with the Lama: (Tib.: Lamai Naljor, Skt.: Guru Yoga) Contains the other two ways

⇨

1. Calming of the mind (Tib.: Shine, Skt.: Shamata)
2. Clear insight (Tib.: Laghtong, Skt.: Vipassana)

↘ ⇧ ↗

Common Start:
The four basic thoughts,
Refuge and the preliminary practices
(Tib. Ngondro)

↗ ⇧ ↘

WAY OF METHODS

SECRET WAY

WAY OF INSIGHT

object of any practice or study, however, is the people: that they can live better, die better, and be reborn better. Here the precious "Phowa" is an outstanding example of a meditation which brings liberation at the moment of death. From 1987 to 1995 I gave this powerful method to over 18,000 around the world, and the Tibetans are amazed by the strength and quickness of our results. Many who thought that one has to live exotic lifestyles in faraway countries to practice the Diamond Way are now busily changing their minds.

Since 1972, so far about 170 Karma Kagyu centers[4] across Eurasia in the Americas and "down under" have been developing a modern access to Buddha's Diamond Way and with great success. Modern Western education, stressing self-reliance and independent thought, proves to be an excellent basis for realizing one's mind, and through such capable groups, celebrating the richness of life and unafraid to use the latest in computers and the Internet, Buddha's most effective teachings are passing into the hands of the most idealistic and independent people worldwide. At this time, holders of the few genuine Buddhist lay and yogi transmissions should consciously aim to introduce their teachings first as new countries become free. There are churches and therapies everywhere for those who want to follow or take their changing feelings seriously, but where else than in no-frills schools of Buddhism shall critical and self-reliant people find a spiritual offer that they must take seriously?

The yogi-view of the Diamond Way guarantees that mind's power will not be suffocated by celibacy, rituals or hierarchy, and that inspired and strong people will find the teachings relevant. It is the responsibility of all who trust in their innate perfection that the teachings stay on the cutting edge of modern life, meaningful to people who question and want experience.

The signs this is progressing well are a healthy sense of humor and people's natural interest in the highest level of teaching they can understand. It is also important that the groups respect others more for what they do and dare and less for the things they omit, for whatever reason that may be. Otherwise there is no certainty that something "living" is transmitted and that not yet another load of "opium for the people" is dumped on the world. Being Buddhist with this attitude means expressing the fearlessness, self-arisen joy, and active compassion of space, and there is no better way to thank the Buddha and no greater benefit for others than to give one's best in whatever one does.

This was a yogi's practical approach to the outer, inner and secret teachings: the Theravada, the Mahayana and the Vajrayana. As became evident at his death, Buddha was totally satisfied with his work. He had passed on everything that beings need for enlightenment. His very last advice to not just believe his words, but to check them out for oneself, explains how this unique and dogma-free gift could develop beings without interruption for the 2,500 years since then.

GOAL OF BUDDHA'S WAYS—
LIBERATION AND ENLIGHTENMENT

Goal of the Small Way—Liberation

The way to liberation consists of two steps. First, one recognizes that there is nothing permanent in the body, just masses of atoms changing place. Then one recognizes that thoughts and feelings have no essence. Although experiences might feel "real" when they occur, only streams of conditions can be found, impermanent and constantly changing.

This insight will grow and increasingly influence one's view of life until it colors all experience. If there is nobody there, then who might get harmed? Understanding there is no self, what can be a target? Insecurity and the feeling of being "outside" are thus abolished, and in pain or difficulty the personal quality of habitually thinking: "I suffer" turns into the general observation that "there is suffering." In all situations one is invulnerable, and there is no better foundation for moving on in one's development. Though the Southern schools of Buddhism consider this level of attainment— Arhatship—the goal to reach in this historical period, to Northern or Mahayana Buddhism it is the natural resting-place before beginning the great voyage of Bodhisattvahood.

The Goal of the Great Way—Enlightenment

Having developed a taste for mind's potential and seeing ever more clearly the unsatisfactory conditions of others, one cannot stop with one's own liberation. Now, enlightenment for the benefit of all becomes the great attraction. The certainty that one's essence cannot be harmed frees power for the complete development of mind. Its fearless all-knowingness, its self-arising joy and active love now beckon. Inseparable from beings' deepest nature, these qualities increase naturally through the removal of mind's second veil, that of stiff ideas. Although it takes thorough work to recognize at all times and places that *what looks through beings' eyes* is radiant space, there exists no more rewarding way to the state of highest functioning and endless happiness.

Yogis often ask their students whether inner experience and outer events are the same as mind, or different from it. Most think the latter, but the answer is both/and. They appear and unfold in mind's space, are experienced by its clarity, and dissolve back into its unlimited essence. They are like waves in the ocean. Are the waves the ocean or are they something else?

From the moment of this recognition, one will limit one's life less with concepts and simply rest in what is. There will be neither distraction when thoughts and feelings manifest, nor sleepiness or confusion if nothing happens. Conscious and at peace in the here and now, the state of pure awareness will bring forth the radiance and unlimited powers of mind.

As formerly mentioned, the removal of mind's veils inevitably produces courage, joy, and active kindness. The understanding that one is neither the body which will die, nor the ever-changing flow of experiences, but indestructible timeless space itself, uproots fear at once. From the level of fearlessness, one experiences whatever happens as the immense richness of space. Birth, death and everything else show the abundance and potential of what may be. Finally, the realization of mind's unlimited quality leads to skillful love. From a position of trust in one's own insight, one acts for the lasting good of beings, undisturbed by political correctness or other passing fads. The message on this level is clear: to neither analyze oneself into non-action nor accept limitations by any of the "isms."

Materialistic thoughts are not a sign that one's meditation is useless. One should see them simply as "practical." Nihilistic thoughts do not mean that one is Nietzsche's reincarnation; one simply recognizes that such thoughts are possible. Existential experiences prove nothing of a lasting nature, and idealistic states of mind may be enjoyed without attachment.

Whatever appears in mind confirms its richness, potential and power. Highest wisdom is always highest functioning and joy! One should let oneself be pleasantly surprised as such states unfold, however. Only beyond hope and fear will enlightened awareness manifest itself.

WIDTH AND DEPTH
OF THE TEACHINGS

THE FOUR CLASSICAL GROUPS

A visit to monasteries and libraries containing the Tibetan *Kanjur* would reveal Buddha's 108 books and 84,000 teachings as categorized into 4 groups of 21,000 each. The first of these aims to remove desire and is called "Vinaya," which contains mainly rules of conduct for monks and nuns. The teachings of "Sutra" diminish anger and ill-will, feelings frequently encountered by the layman during the give and take of everyday life. The "Abhidharma" is for the fortunate few who have a surplus for thinking about the world, and cuts the root of confusion and unclear thinking. These first three sections are learned in school-like situations and with the same disadvantage: information moves slowly from the head to the heart, from thoughts to experience.

The fourth part, however, touches the totality of beings. One may compare it to riding a fast motorcycle or falling deeply in love. It fundamentally changes people, awakens all inner powers, and is called "Vajrayana" or "The Diamond Way." Through its exceedingly skillful methods, people have reached not only liberation but Buddhahood in a single lifetime.

Whether Mahamudra belongs inside the Diamond Way or stands on its own is still debated by the wise and learned. Both viewpoints make sense. Though unlimited like Maha Ati in its view, Mahamudra influences both the basis and way and is the goal itself. Whoever wants to use the term "tantra" for the part of the Diamond Way which works with imagination, breathing, sexuality and form, must always say "Buddhist tantra" (the word "Tantra" comes from "weaving" and denotes experiences which become an inseparable part of one). This is because the Hindus use the same term for their secret teachings, which are something fundamentally different. Though many images and expressions may appear similar at first glance, both way and goal are different. The Hindu seeks strength (Shakti), which is the point from where Buddhists begin, while the Buddhist goal is ultimate wisdom, Jnana (Skt.) or Yeshe (Tib.). Also, the system of inner channels in the body (through the spine or in its middle) and the position of the energy-wheels is different. Mixing these systems is, like the old texts say, a grievous mistake.

Right understanding and practice of the Diamond Way makes one truly great. It lifts the student from the level of the "poor man" and the limiting view of "either/or" to the experience of the "rich man": the all-encompassing "both/and." Here, the potential of unlimited space is the constant source of reference. One elegantly catches the "mole" of the ordinary mind, puts contact lenses on its eyes, ties wings to its paws, glues feathers onto its tail and sends it into the sky as an eagle. Beyond all mental fabrications, everything is then eternally fresh and new.

GOING THE WAY "ALONE"

The popular Western concept of going to enlightenment "alone" comes in statistically a very poor third after the quick success of a full practice with a teacher or group and the much more painstaking approach of progressive study. Though it sounds so attractive to a modern person who feels in control of his life to become enlightened by oneself, there are just too many pitfalls. Learning about mind is much more intricate than studying outer phenomena, and there are always the lurking enemies of pride and dislike that may derail one's growth. Especially the attempt to rediscover and hold on to drug-induced "highs" through Buddhist meditation never pays off. Though highest unchanging joy is the result of these methods, they are based on an opposite and timeless approach: the experience of mind itself and not of its many projections.

Actually, it should not be difficult to opt for the way of lasting results. The Buddha is never moralistic or heavy, and the goal of the teaching is only to make beings independent, through giving them access to mind's possibilities. Also the process of learning is nothing revolutionary. In life one learns even simpler things than that from others. Whoever will try to become enlightened on their own, I advise to first make a good foundation. By avoiding words and actions which harm, one diminishes the causes for later trouble. Also a deep motivation is needed, such as wishing everyone the best, and the intelligence and inner space to not take things personally.

The highest level, however, cannot be properly understood and is impossible to maintain without a teacher. If the communication is missing which neutralizes pride, sentimentality and superficiality, one may become lonely or useless in daily life. On this level, it is no exaggeration to warn against the dangers of going alone. Firstly, one is at the mercy of books which are often inadequately translated, and therefore one cannot distinguish the different teachings. Secondly, even authentic Buddhist sources use different terminology which is also confusing. Finally, when one has made it well to the great highway towards enlightenment, two major obstacles still lurk, which one may not easily recognize as such.

On one hand, there are tempting exits from the rigor of holding the highest view: the so-called "soft" sciences.

Though it makes sense to employ the spiritual capacities one develops, such as intuition or healing, if they become a substitute for the final goal—enlightenment for the benefit of all—they waste one's precious opportunity for realizing timeless values.

Also, the psychic experiences so warmly greeted on one's way may be veiled hindrances; appearing due to conditions, there is no way they can stay. If, however, one tries to carry along these milestones of development, soon one will have arms like a gorilla and be too loaded with concepts to reach mind's effortless state. Only beyond hope and fear will one's enlightened qualities freely unfold. It is much wiser to trust the spontaneous richness of mind to supply whatever enlightened qualities are needed along the way, than to expect or cling to glimpses one once had. Whoever practices with such confidence will not stop wondering how boundless everything is.

BUDDHISM TODAY

In Tibet, there were three possible ways of following Buddhism: one might become a monk, practice as a lay person, or be a yogi. Monks and nuns lived separately in monasteries and nunneries and had strict rules of conduct. The lay people had families, a normal occupation, and tried to put the teachings into their everyday lives. The yogis lived unrestricted by social norms, often in various caves with changing partners, and focused their whole lives on spiritual development (one example is the well known yogi, Milarepa).

Since today people in the developed countries have the means to decide about the number of their offspring, there will be no large Buddhist monasteries. The reason for men and women to live separately in earlier times was not that

Buddha was prudish, or that his teachings were hostile to the body. Nor did he have a fear of future heirs to contest accumulated wealth like the Catholic church, but people simply could not make love without having children and family life restricted their time for study and meditation. The vows of monks and nuns were gathered from Buddha's advice to various followers and groups, and though much looks strange in a modern setting, they cannot be changed to fit new situations.

In the West, however, the originally separate groups of yogis and lay people are coming very close. As there is no need for the former to compete with the red-robed monks and nuns in obtaining the support of the productive population, they also don't need the outer props which formerly made them easily distinguishable, like flowing white robes and wild hair styles. This reduces the distance from the lay people of today who on their side are so freely backed by a welfare state that they no longer need to establish vast families for looking after them in old age. My students around the world seem to bridge and unite the best of both ways. In their daily lives they generally hold the Mahamudra, a yogi's liberating view, while accomplishing whatever is expected for a productive and meaningful life. Only during holidays does the traditional yogi style manifest outwardly, as many move their tents from one meditation course to the next.

Two thousand five hundred and fifty years ago in India, many people seem to have been attracted to Buddha's advice about cause and effect. Less, apparently, wished to hear about wisdom and compassion, and only a few had the conditions for the pure view of the Diamond Way. Today in the West, with plenty of gifted people and good karma around, many wish to experience the space-clarity of mind while they prefer to leave questions of cause and effect to the police: whether they managed to catch someone or not. Also, philosophy and psychology only have minor pull, since most have been fed these subjects in uninspired ways in school. Modern, self-confident people want direct experience.

The Western Framework of the Teachings

Whoever supports Buddha's teachings is a link in their unbroken chain. Whether this happens through giving money for the Centers to run, as a local or a traveling teacher, or as an example to society, family and friends, one should know as much Buddhism as possible. Even those who prefer working with beings on a one-by-one basis will see their effectiveness grow vastly when they obtain a view of the whole path and can choose among its wide range of methods. With sufficient insight, one can stabilize peoples' development and convey a joyful anticipation of the levels ahead. For such practical aims, however, the institutional separation of the teachings into Vinaya, Sutra, Abhidharma and Vajrayana is too remote. Here, one needs a practice-oriented approach to their richness. Before embarking on that, however, a few words to all hopefuls who plan a massive assault on the frustrations of conditioned existence: one needs a long breath.

Even though the world offers increasing numbers of glossy ways to attain spiritual experiences, reality is far from that. The karmic habitual energies of beings are of a sticky quality, and few have the necessary basis for even starting on a path—which is the certainty that they possess a mind and can work with it to obtain lasting results. Today this means understanding that mind is not produced by the impermanent brain but transformed by it; that its stream of information moves since beginningless time from one conditioned existence to the next, picking up the experiences which mature as one's next life . . . that this goes on until one recognizes the mirror behind the pictures, mind's unconditioned state. The veils covering one's consciousness exist since beginningless time, and are no weak opponent. Even with the strongest of blessing and meditations, their removal must happen step by step.

Among today's confusing variety of teachers, one may actually recognize a good Lama or Buddhist author by the fact that he points to transforming methods. He does not try to please his students by talking sweetly around difficult subjects, leaving them with the superficial satisfactions of having their exotic or preconceived ideas confirmed but with little or no real guidance. Even Lamas of the three "old" Tibetan lineages, who have the power to zap their students with the Mahamudra or Dzog Chen, the Buddha's ultimate teaching, should quickly recommend the practical way to achieve that state: the not-so-glorious "foundational practices," such as the seemingly endless repetitions called the Ngondro. These practices help produce the subconscious richness and purifications which are the only lasting basis for joy.

"Higher practices" are thus self-secret and only become relevant when their foundation has been accomplished in this or an earlier life. Also, as a body in itself represents a lot of inertia, each subsequent physical form must have its channels of wisdom opened up, a painstaking process. The beginning of a being's spiritual search is a quest for happiness, and the discovery that is produced by useful thoughts, words and actions. Thus, one starts working practically with cause and effect. The improved feedback both from the external world and from one's own subconscious gradually liberates mind's wealth, and, manifesting as compassion and inspired wisdom, such motivation will guide body and speech to further benefit others. From a foundation of so much good, a strong attraction towards mind's full potential will arise as well as devotion towards those having realized it: these feelings constitute a very fast lane to enlightenment. Each of the three levels mentioned fits a type of human being: the egocentric, the altruistic, and the yogi. And all need three supports for their unfoldment, the pillars of "knowledge with questions," "meditation," and "holding the level."

Knowledge—Meditation—Holding the Level

Whatever knowledge or insight one might wish to gain, one must first know the conditions. Clear teachings relevant to one's life must be combined with a chance to check them practically, unhindered by any dogmas or articles of faith. Whether one wishes to have an undisturbed existence, live a world of rich inner experience, or grow massively to become a Buddha among Buddhas: one must have right understanding and a chance to clarify doubts. Buddha's very last words show that he wanted this. After his much quoted statement that he could die happily, having given all the advice that benefits beings, he added something that makes his example perfect for our times. "Now, don't believe anything just because a Buddha told you, but check everything for yourselves. See if the teachings fit with your experience and be your own guiding lights." As science gets more Buddhist with every new discovery, making the following statement may be risk free: if there were a point where the teachings were evidently wrong, and science right, one should trust science. Buddha himself would want this.

The middle pillar stands for meditation. Having such strong effects, especially on the level of the Diamond Way, practice-oriented methods should be given under the right circumstances by an authorized teacher or a group practicing under his guidance. Understanding needs to mature and thoughts deepen into experience. After obstacles have been removed and right view established, a realization of the main points concerning the emptiness and interdependence of all phenomena will bring the naturally dwelling mind to manifest clear awareness and attractive power.

The third pillar consolidates attainment. Nothing is less convincing, for oneself or others, than insecurity or moodiness. Therefore, the pillar of "holding whatever state has been attained" is essential. On the three levels respectively, it protects against harmful actions, anger, or losing the highest view.

THE HOUSE OF BUDDHA'S TEACHINGS

Mahamudra
Union of Basis, Way and Goal

	1. Knowledge	2. Meditation	3. Holding the Level	
Vajrayana The Diamond Way	Buddha as mirror of mind's essence	Union with enlightenment through mind's energy, awareness, or devotion	Holding the pure view/ highest truth and functioning = highest joy. Never losing that state	Yogis C
Mahayana The Great Way	Inner practice Developing compassion and wisdom in balance.	Experience of emptiness, strengthening of compassionate motivation	Avoidance of anger. Bodhisattva vow	Altruists B
Theravada The Small Way	Outer practice Working with cause and effect.	Calming mind to create a distance.	Avoiding harmful actions, external vows	Self-centered people A

On the level of practice, Buddha's teachings may thus be compared to a building of three stories held by three columns, all under the roof of Mahamudra (see table below). They are meant to offer egocentrics, altruists and yogis the necessary knowledge, method and strength on their ways. The following table counts the columns as 1,2,3 and the levels as A, B, C.

A. The Level of One's Own Benefit

1. Knowledge

If the focus is on one's own happiness, then one needs to know about cause and effect. Though the factors leading to joy or pain should not be too difficult to understand—given the complexity of so much else that people learn—the more events "come to life," the less ones' intelligence seems to function. Therefore, probably everyone can benefit from an occasional drill to make body, speech and mind better sources of lasting happiness. On Buddha's way this is, of course, entirely voluntary. Unlike religions of faith, humorless in their preoccupation with commanding what should be avoided, it is relieving that he gave not one order, only advice, and that he always stresses the positive side. Everyone has to circumvent enough rules, be they traffic or whatever, to get on with life, and Buddha's way is thus attractive to the self-reliant. As he is fully a man and not working for any alien force or god, it is not difficult to trust him. He wants colleagues, not followers, and his only objective is our enlightenment. No unhealthy fear of joy or sexuality twists his message, and his general advice on this first level is to perceive one's body, speech and mind as tools.

The body may protect, share love, or be otherwise generous. The advice concerning physical love, of course, omits monks and nuns.

Speech—communication—can help beings develop, bring them inner peace, show them the richness of the world, and make them understand others. There is great meaning in using the possibilities of life with maximum awareness.

Where mind is concerned, Buddha advises wishing all beings the best. One should appreciate the good done by others, even try to outdo them for the common good, and always remember cause and effect. As today's thoughts will find words tomorrow and lead to actions later, this knowledge is essential.

2. Meditation

Meditation turns accepted information into experience. On the first level, its purpose is to calm the mind and keep it in one place. It creates space between the experiencer and his experiences, permitting the wise to choose roles in the comedies of life and avoid its tragedies. This protective distance is most frequently achieved through awareness of one's breath, a meditation called "Shamatha" in Sanskrit and "Shine" in Tibetan. Whoever can hold this state of mind in the lab situation of one's meditation, will gradually accomplish the same in daily life. This is a first step in one's development and a necessary foundation for both penetrating insight and more elaborate practices.

3. Holding the level

To protect his students from losing this security, Buddha gave the so-called "outer" vows. They concern actions that are better avoided and contain an impressive two hundred fifty-four things which monks cannot do and about three hundred fifty restrictions on nuns. Being his advice to various celibate groups to make them better examples to society and live together with less friction, they address unusual lifestyles and mainly concern themselves with blocking the sexual urge. To a lay person in the give and take of a full life, only a few outer vows have any meaning, and one should only take what one really wishes to keep. Traditionally, these mean not to kill any large being, to steal or to lie seriously to harm others, or by misrepresenting one's spiritual experiences. Furthermore, it is useful not to abuse "dulling" chemicals such as drugs or alcohol, and to decide against sexually harming others, breaking hearts unnecessarily, or whatever. The interpretation of the last point Buddha kept very wide to permit his lay students to thrive in very varied cultures. It always includes incest, however, probably to protect the gene pool. Some yogis take outer vows while others do not.

The "outer" vows must be distinguished from commandments given by Christian or Hindu traditions and are the total opposite of the Muslim Sharia which prescribes barbaric punishments, such as stonings for female infidelity, or chopping off peoples' limbs for theft. Buddha only wants beings to do well. There is no other reason for any practice or vow and, if no longer wanted, one may simply return them to the giver with the protection that they offer. Learning to fully trust Buddha's view on the body should start here because it may not come easily. Especially those damaged by moralizing religions often have difficulty simply relaxing and believing their good luck. As explained in the highest teachings, Buddha sees the physical body as a temple of light. It has seventy two thousand channels filled with enlightened energy, and its separate parts as well as their functions are meaningful and essentially pure.

This first level of vows makes sense because causality guides the world. If not purified, all thoughts, words, and actions will bring future results. Taking the vows protects one by reminding one of this fact.

B. The Level of Altruists

1. Knowledge

Work done on the first level brings increasingly agreeable feedback, both from one's surroundings and from one's own store-consciousness. Under such conditions, mind develops additional qualities. When less energy is needed for inner and outer entanglements, the surplus arising expresses itself as wisdom and compassion. The three levels of compassion have been mentioned already, and one may be kind as a king, putting oneself in a strong position before sharing; as a rower, taking others along; or as a shepherd, thinking of others first. One should do what comes naturally, but as the trick is to forget one's illusion of a "self," the shepherd reaches the goal first.

Enlightened wisdom shines through ever new cracks in the crumbling walls of disturbing emotions and stiff concepts. Whoever experiences the world as an individual dream inside a collective one, which it is, while not forgetting cause and effect, will be able to help countless beings. Buddha's teaching on the Bodhisattva mind and emptiness belong here.

2. Meditation

Meditation on the second level means resting in compassionate space. Here, one's motivation becomes a major part of the absorption. Meditations of this kind begin with the wish to attain enlightenment for the benefit of all beings and finish by sharing one's accumulated inner wealth. Early on the way, actions will not reach far, but as one's powers grow, the motivation already developed will direct them towards the long-range good of all.

3. Holding the level

Protecting one's inner life and adding to mind's richness means controlling the disturbing feelings. Here, anger is the biggest obstacle of all and in this battle, all weapons should be used. It is best to continuously remove the soil from the root of ill will by not giving the feeling any attention.

Until a few years ago, this part of Buddha's advice—to not give attention to negative states—was far from current psychological views, and certain groups resist it strongly still today. But if one compares vintage therapists and feminists to time-worn Buddhists, or watches the growing crowds of singles and their fears, it becomes evident that the Buddhist handling of anger brings stable happiness and real courage. Even though people should protect their precious time and cut through long-winded personal trips much more decisively than is usually done, still the feeling of anger—fresh as well as seasoned—is never useful and blocks all growth.

During the last few decades, much of the civilized world has blamed first the Russians, then imperialism, society, and finally dominating mothers for peoples' problems. Right now the focus is on child-molesting uncles, but the attitude of placing the fault with others makes everybody weak. Whether one likes it or not, the law of cause and effect excludes nobody. What uncles may do to one now, one surely did to them in former lives, and one can only avoid future bad meetings by decisively stopping what is harmful in oneself, starting anew without anger, and wishing whoever harms others better mental health. The mature view holds agreeable experiences to be blessings, while everything difficult is seen as training and purification. Knowing no judging god or fate as the cause of beings' sufferings, but only ignorance and negative actions which were not neutralized in time, Buddhism advises employing all available means of behavior and meditation to remove future suffering and help others through any experience one gains.

C. The Level of Yogis

A few general observations about way and goal always make sense. Before entering the Diamond Way, the most exciting part of Buddha's teachings, it is useful to remind oneself that mind's unchanging quality is awareness. Perfection is everybody's natural state and manifests through a very simple process. The way computers do everything with the numbers 0 and 1, two steps of growth repeat themselves until enlightenment: the accumulation of positive impressions and the development of wisdom. Kind thoughts, words, and actions pacify mind, bringing forth liberating insights, and such pleasant feedback again motivates one to do more good. As beyond-personal awareness shines ever stronger, it becomes painfully evident how all beings chase joy and try to avoid suffering but usually seek their bliss in conditioned situations where no lasting happiness can be found. Realizing how personally unenlightened beings take their feelings, and how strongly all are hostage to them, one will naturally protect them. Focusing rather on people's long-term needs than on their passing wishes—be they political or whatever—one will be more than a fair-weather friend.

Accumulating positive impressions that lead to wisdom, which in turn produces more good, is thus the "way." Finally everything will fit; wherever one looks, there will be only purity. There is then only happiness within, and fulfillment without. From a position of such richness, mind joyfully goes beyond concepts and trusts in its timeless space; in this state freed of hope and fear, every breakthrough makes one more spontaneous and effortless. However, one still has to watch out: what is left of one's illusion of "self" will try to harness any experience to its ongoing horse-trading. Producing thoughts such as, "My clear light lasted longer than his last week," or "Now, I shall soon be enlightened," stains the freshness of experience and makes conscientious meditators believe they have fallen down. In reality, however, such thoughts are meaningless. If one gives them no power, they can do nothing. Staying ever longer in mind's clear light, subject, object and action become one, and it is no longer possible to lose this state.

1. Knowledge

Seeing things as mutually conditioned, constantly changing and not truly existent, such as they actually are, while at the same time accumulating vast quantities of positive impressions, leads one to the level of yogis. This invariably brings about enlightenment. Insight on this level goes beyond concepts. Here, Buddha is not seen as a god or something "outside" but as a constant mirror to one's mind. He expresses a perfectly attractive essence that one can entirely trust. As disturbing feelings, veils of confusion, and clumsy habits are no longer taken seriously and thus diminish, this state is recognized as somehow deeply familiar.

Having arrived on this third level and protected by unbroken bonds to one's teacher, the unshakable experience mentioned above will solidify. The understanding that experiencer, object experienced and act of experiencing are mutually conditioned and truly one becomes certainty. Freeing all mind's power, this is enlightenment and the final goal.

2. Meditation

When Buddha's students shared this understanding, he taught them three approaches. Starting with the Foundational Practices or Ngondro, all ultimately lead to the realization of mind's natural purity. As the wealth of psychological and philosophical wisdom employed on each of these ascents of the Diamond Way is so unique, amazing, and at the same time so little known, here is an extensive presentation.

Buddha's "path of methods" contains countless tools and is for people of a practical bent. He empowered them by either radiating out the single Buddha-forms of the three lower classes of Tantra or by changing his own body into the highest united aspects. Looking like holograms, but radiant with limitless energy, the feedback from the colors, positions, attributes and invocations (Mantras) of these light-forms brings forth various enlightened qualities.

Kriya, Charya and Yoga are the names of the first Tantra levels, and meditating on their single forms gradually strengthens beings' confidence in their Buddha-nature. Mind's full expression of its space and joy, however, only manifests as the peaceful or protective united forms of the Anuttarayogatantra. These male-female aspects in union alone contain all aspects of enlightenment, and meditating on them can bring complete realization in one life.

Even though one may immediately meditate on the "close" forms of a lineage which are embodied by one's teacher, it is of great value to also take the permission (lung), the empowerment (wang),[5] or the guided meditation (bum lung),[6] from a street-wise lama who keeps his style, and will cause no later embarrassment. Seeds thus planted in one's store-consciousness will grow, and most ascribe a real change or deepening of absorption to such ceremonies. If it is additionally understood that one is meeting aspects of the mind's inherent perfection, such rituals constitute one's entry into a pure land. Many strongly experience the daily informal transmissions of Mahamudra from their lama, and everybody can follow a guided meditation in one's own language, but as so few know what the occasional giver of a formal initiation chants and does with his instruments, here follows a short description of this process as it has been handed down.

After a symbolic purification, a presentation of the text read in Tibetan, the bribing of bad energies to make them leave, and the giving of refuge, the point where the receiver becomes active is during the first or "vase" initiation. Touching people's heads with a vase and sometimes letting them drink the nectar from it, the lama here transmits the power to experience one's body as the light form of the Buddha invoked. In the second or "secret" initiation one repeats the key vibrations—heart-mantras—of these forms to open one's inner channels and share their energies. The third or "wisdom insight" initiation conveys the joy of yogic union, bringing together compassion and wisdom, joy and space, while the fourth and highest, the so-called "word" initiation, introduces one to the ultimate state of Mahamudra. Here, the teacher's space-awareness unites with one's own, and one partakes in mind's timeless state.

Thus, if one removes the cultural Tibetan frame, initiations work like guided meditations or blessings. Their texts may well be described as invocations, which are interrupted at certain points to transmit the built-up enlightened energies. Above all, they introduce one to mind's timeless, limitless insight, which is the only refuge. Afterwards, if one's awareness is linked to a pure land, sound is heard ever more as mantra, and every form is increasingly seen as meaningful, while any mental activity is recognized as the playful brilliance of mind. This highest view totally protects its holders, and its blessing filters down and also influences the levels of altruists and egocentrics. If we are all Buddhas in pure lands, it is only natural to express compassion and wisdom, and any premeditated harm to others is totally out—except to teach them a lesson.

Such complete tools for the mind—if given by a capable yogi who transparently acts as he teaches—not only boost one's inner development. The invoked energy fields stay active around one and transform the outer world into a teacher. The protectors[7] especially make themselves felt. Even before one may consciously think of them, one is already noticeably surrounded by their energy field. The mere thought of a mantra condenses the activity of the respective Buddha out of space, and the repeated melting-together when meditating will gradually bring an absorption of their eminent qualities. Identifying with the enlightened Buddha-forms, until one has become them, is the "way of methods."

The "way of insight" is more relevant to today's busy life style and short vacations, but requires more time. It was also brought to Tibet by Marpa nine hundred and fifty years ago and is much more intricate than many people would like to believe. It certainly needs the support of an experienced teacher. This way, too, is best entered after the Foundational Practices (Ngondro), because the vast accumulation of positive impressions built up through their massive repetitions safeguard against the dangerous "white wall" effect, where mistaken pacifying meditations rob mind of its power. Confused "self-taught" meditators and overly adjusted groups are warning examples. Quality, not quantity, is the key here: short periods of real awareness interrupted by phases of relaxation and ample teachings on the nature of mind. Whoever just sits for hours on end will become dull, and mind's natural freshness will be lost. The meditations which hold and pacify mind are known as "Shine" in Tibetan and "Shamatha" in Sanskrit, leading to the penetrating insight called "Lhagtong" or "Vipassana." Its simplest form consists of observing the flow of breath at the tip of one's nose without any judgment, and on its highest level one's body, speech and mind are experienced as those of one's teacher or closest Buddha-aspect, while one rests naturally in his pure land.

Though both meditation on the Buddha-aspects and staying in penetrating insight bring immense growth, the most direct way to realize one's lama's qualities are the Guru Yogas, as practiced in the Karma Kagyu centers around the world.

This is the essence of the Kagyü transmission and, from the yogis of India up to today, one sees students realizing their full potential in the stream of their teachers' blessing. Here is an example from when Buddhism was brought to Tibet the second time.

The day when Marpa sat in front of Naropa, nine hundred years ago, Naropa's Buddha Aspect Hevajra—Kye Dorje—appeared at his side, as big as a house and with many arms. He was in standing union with Dagmema, his consort, and they radiated like a thousand suns.

Marpa was of course deeply impressed and Naropa, who probably looked like any old Indian, asked him: Now you see him and me, whom will you greet first? Marpa's reasoning was quite understandable; he bowed towards the Yidam, but Naropa laughed. "Mistake," he said, "with us the Lama is everything." He dissolved the vast energy-field into a rainbow and absorbed it into his heart.

Today, this rapid method of growth works very effectively in the Karma Kagyü groups. As the power field involved on one's way is the nature of highest wisdom, after refuge one may be certain that everything pleasant is a blessing, and that everything difficult removes later suffering and is a useful teaching on how to benefit others.

Because a full identification on the level of perfection presses countless "enlightenment buttons" in one's subconscious, it is a very fast way to realize one's original awareness. Here, the mutually conditioned, dependently originating nature of things is clearly recognized—a precondition to the ultimate insight that seer, seeing and object seen are inseparable parts of the same totality.

Through whichever means one may enter, however, the Mahamudra is unique. Its view effortlessly blends the *basis*—the Buddha-nature of all beings—with the *way* to its joyful discovery and thus brings about the *goal* of full enlightenment. All concepts fade when it is imparted, and it especially provides those with basic confidence a fast lane to enlighten-

ment. The intensity of experience on this highest level irons
out anything stilted in one's expression, and the self-liberation
of all dualistic processes becomes completely natural. Beyond
any doubt, the Mahamudra demonstrates mind's space, clarity, and limitlessness to be the only reality. The resultant
insight, that it is much more important not to be disturbed by
thoughts or feelings than to judge them, liberates masses of
energy in everyone. The ocean is simply so much more
important than its waves.

Buddha directed his highest teachings to those mainly
influenced by their desires. These methods rely on beings'
own experience and the wealth of mind's free play. Their
formless aspect is then called Mahamudra or Chag-Chen, and
the same kind of people take naturally to the "Mother"
Tantras. These methods are the specialty of the Kagyu lineage.
If people have dominant anger or pride, the view of mind's
self-liberating quality—that it will all go away again—is
stressed in the Maha-Ati or Dzog-Chen, and the "Father"
Tantras are the best approach. This part is much taught by the
Nyingmapas or "old" Tibetan school. Through their total or
"tantric" view, these two lineages transform body, speech, and
mind with countless methods for quick enlightenment. The
Madhyamaka or Uma Chenpo contains a similar level of
theory but from Buddha's *Sutras* and essentially removes
ignorance and confusion. It is the main practice of the
Gelugpa or "virtuous" school, the state church which gov-
erned Tibet. Since the motor for one's development is the
intellect, however, it is a much slower path. The Buddha-
Family most directly transforming ignorance is the "Non-
dual," and, as may be experienced today with the 17th
Karmapa, Thaye Dorje, in the free world as well as from
sources such as the Mahamudra-texts of his various incarna-
tions, one fine teacher and school may embody all of the
above.

3. Holding the level

One major decision maintains this highest realization and secures the whole framework of one's growth: that one will never leave the pure realms again. In Buddhism this does not involve mere "positive thinking," which means clinging to what is beautiful and willfully missing out on suffering. Here, it is the mirror which is important, the experiencer, and not the gods, demons or other images coming and going there. On this level, one knows in the very marrow of one's bones that the highest truth is the highest joy, and one experiences mind as fearless and rich, as naturally compassionate and powerful. The recognition, that whatever happens or doesn't happen are expressions of mind's unlimited clear light, removes all tightness, and the knowledge that one's true essence is indestructible brings real and lasting security. From here on, one is at home in whatever happens. Having understood that one is neither the body that will become sick, old and die, nor the thoughts that change all the time, one becomes that which looks through one's eyes and listens through one's ears, right here and now: aware, limitless space. It is totally beyond any coming and going, beyond birth and death.

On this level of fearlessness, everything is the free play of mind. Appearance as well as disappearance only shows its unlimited richness. One no longer needs to hope for a good film; one owns the cinema and can play what one wants. What is being acted out is now less relevant; the important point is that the screen has no holes and that the projector works. When mind's radiant energy no longer restricts itself through attachment or aversion, all phenomena, outer as well as inner, will manifest as fresh and exciting just because they can take place. From this state of freedom, one's experience will be like this: "A few days ago I was jealous, then I became angry, and right now I am confused. How exciting, let's see what

tomorrow brings!" while all the time continuing in an uncon-
cerned way with whatever meaningful activity lies in front of
one. Acting from much certainty and richness, mind's awareness of its unlimited quality will bring actions of real and long-
term benefit for all, whatever the collective confusion or
"political correctness" of the times may prescribe. Today, for
instance, every human equipped with reason should insist on
limiting the birth rates in the ghettos and poor countries of the
world.

As a sure sign of inner growth, the wish for egotistical joys
will gradually disappear. This happens both because the
permanent bliss of full awareness goes far beyond any
conditioned experience, its very intensity dissolving any
illusion of a separate "self," and because everybody so
obviously receives everything in life from others. Seeing that,
what other feeling could one foster towards them than
gratitude? Choosing this motivation means behaving like a
Buddha until one becomes one, and possessing real power,
one does not need to follow popular views.

Evidently, the speed of one's arrival depends on the
method employed. On may dig a hole with one's hand, a
shovel or a dredge, and walk, drive or fly to enlightenment. If
one chooses the first by mainly avoiding the causes of one's
own suffering, the process is repetitive. It concerns things one
should have learned already as a child, and is not very
inspiring.

On the second level, compassion and wisdom are the
guide. If they are kept in balance, the outcome will be good.
Important at this point is one's attention to intuition and to
feedback from the world. Here one has to examine one's own
mind frequently. If egotistical thoughts increase, compassion
for others must be diminishing and the world will soon
become difficult. If one finds stiff ideas multiplying, the lack
of immediate experience will quickly make one irrelevant.

The third and ultimate step depends on one's view. Here all one needs to observe is the level of awareness: is the feeling in every experience growth, purity, and freshness? Does one see the potential Buddha in others and oneself? If the answer is "yes," inner wealth and meaning can only grow, and the world will manifest steadily deeper levels of inherent perfection.

Nothing is more important than consolidating the above experience. Even though the understanding of "non-ego" as developed in Southern Buddhism means liberation and an end to suffering, this view only brings some of mind's capacities into play. Its realization takes countless lifetimes, and one stays vulnerable until the end, if lacking the strong protection afforded by compassion. That noble feeling, combined with beyond-personal insight into the emptiness and dreamlike nature of all phenomena, is the reason why Northern Buddhism is so well-rounded, flexible and practical.

Only the Diamond-Way, however, uses all the capacities of body, speech, and mind, and employs beings' sexuality, fantasy, and courage on their way. From the construction crane of highest confidence—the view of natural purity—it first lays the necessary foundation of right actions, then places the walls of motivation and wisdom, and finally positions the roof of enlightened view. Correctly understood, the yogi-level thus already contains the Mahamudra.

The Mahamudra

As already seen, the Mahamudra (Tib.: Chag Chen) begins with the accumulation of inner richness and a deep trust in one's teacher who—fearless, joyful and hard working—needs to visibly embody the state of perfection. When the students have stored enough positive impression in their minds to no longer be dependent on happiness from elsewhere, the resultant state is called "one-pointedness." It is sometimes described as the condition "where mind stays where one's behind is," or one may compare it to having an exciting girlfriend and a fridge full of food. Why should one want to leave?

Out of this surplus arises the non-artificial state. Seeing ever more clearly how the here and now is much more meaningful than any mental fabrication, one will stop playing games. This deep honesty is in no way superficial, and it includes peoples' outer, inner, and secret levels. Even today, where old-fashioned physical inhibitions like shame of one's body or sexuality are rare in free countries, people still are not really spontaneous and have difficulty bringing their speech and mind into line. Being totally direct and without contradiction in every situation, non-artificiality goes beyond anything contrived. It constitutes a perfect and unshakable level of realization in itself.

Reaching the third state of "one taste" means a massive leap on one's way to enlightenment. Here, the inner light of awareness pervades all experience with such strength and clarity that it can no longer be lost. During the finest moments in love-making, when negotiating fast curves on one's motorcycle, or in the free fall before one's parachute opens, the non-Buddhist also has brief but real experiences of this state, but when reached through the power of mind itself, the vast richness of space will remain an unbroken experience.

The term for the fourth and highest realization is actually a joke, but on the Buddha-level, nothing is complicated or heavy. It is called "non-meditation," which doesn't mean staying on one's couch. Here one acts spontaneously to whatever arises. Where the full potential of space is known, and one sees clearly the situation of all beings, every action, word, or thought will bring relative as well as lasting benefit.

Giving and taking freely, one joyfully "rides the tiger" of highest insight.

This book contains the view I pass on to my students today and is the basis for the teaching and lifestyle shared by growing numbers of lay Buddhists around the world. Based on transparency, friendship, and a critical intelligence, groups with such fine people now bring the full range of Buddhism into the West. Inspiring others to also act like Buddhas—fearlessly, joyfully, and with active love—they will automatically accomplish the four steps of Mahamudra mentioned above. This could mean you! Much luck and perseverance.

MEDITATIONS

The following practices cover a progressive range of Buddhist meditations, all employing enlightened feedback through imagination and "form." As you move through them step by step, at some point your main focus will become evident, and that is the level to work from. Except for the Guru-Yoga, the full power of which will only manifest when you have received my transmission, you may guide meditations for others when you feel comfortable with them yourselves.

The first meditations increase generally enjoyable human qualities in the practitioner, and the Guru-Yoga permits a direct identification with enlightenment. With one's growing recognition that nothing "physical" melts together in the phase of uniting with the Buddhas, but that inner and outer awareness meet, one will effortlessly bring the fearlessness, joy, and love of that state into the world.

Meditation on Light and Breath
(general meditation)

We sit comfortably, whether on a pillow or on a chair. Our hands rest in our lap, the right on top of the left, palms up and thumbs lightly touching. We keep our back straight without tightness, and our chin pulled in a little.

First we calm our mind. We feel the formless stream of air which comes and goes at the tip of our nose, letting thoughts and sounds go by without holding on to them.

Now we will meditate in order to experience mind and to gain a distance from our disturbing emotions. Only then can we really be useful to others.

A foot-and-a-half in front of our nose, there now appears a clear transparent light. While we breathe in, the light moves in a stream down through the center of our body. On its way, the clear light turns ever more red. Stopping briefly four fingers below the navel, the transparent light has become totally red. When we exhale naturally, the red light moves upward and becomes gradually more blue. A foot and a half in front of us, the blue transparent light again becomes clear and we inhale it once more. We hold this awareness without tension, while our breath comes and goes naturally.

If it is difficult to see the colors, we simply think them: clear light when we inhale, red light when the light stops below the navel, and blue when we exhale.

After a while we may also focus on the vibrations of our breath. While inhaling, we hear the syllable **OM.**

While holding the light below the navel, we hear a deep **AH,** *and while exhaling, we hear the vibration of* **HUNG.**

We stay with this for as long as we like.

At the end of the meditation, the world appears fresh and new. We wish that all the good which just happened may become limitless, radiate out to all beings everywhere, remove their suffering, and give them the only lasting joy, the realization of the nature of mind.

Rainbow Meditation
(general meditation)

We sit relaxed and straight, our right hand resting in our left palm and our thumbs lightly touching. If not seated in a chair, our right calf rests on or in front of the left one, and we draw our chin slightly in.

First, we calm the mind. We feel the formless stream of air, coming and going at the tip of our nose, and let thoughts and noises pass without evaluation.

Then we want to meditate, to experience mind's richness, and gain distance from any disturbing emotion. Not until then can one really help others.

At the heart-level in the center of our chest, there now appears a tiny rainbow light. Gradually it expands through our body, totally filling it, and dissolving all diseases and obstacles on its way. When we can stay with this awareness, our body shines like a lamp and light streams in all directions, filling space. It dissolves the suffering of beings everywhere, and the world now shines with great meaning and joy. All are in a pure land, full of limitless possibilities. Everything is self-liberating. We emanate this light as long as it feels natural.

When we end this meditation, the light returns and absorbs the outer world into open space. It shines into our bodies, which also dissolve, and there is now only awareness, with no form, center, or end.

Then, like a fish jumping from the water, again a world appears. Everything vibrates with meaning, all beings are perfect in essence, and our body and speech are tools for benefiting others. Finally, we wish that all the conscious good which happened may become limitless and stream out to everybody, and that it will remove their suffering and bring them the only lasting joy: the recognition of the nature of mind.

Meditation on Giving and Taking
(Meditation of the Great Way)

Though one's ability to benefit others may at present be limited, meditations of this kind create a strong motivation not to forget them when the power arises. It is thus effective against egotism and spiritual pride.

We feel the formless stream of air coming and going at the tip of our nose and let thoughts and sounds pass without evaluation.

When mind is calm, we take refuge in Buddha as our goal, in his teachings which bring us there, and in our friends on the way. From this meditation we wish the power to benefit beings by understanding the conditioned nature of all things.

Now we experience the suffering of all beings as black clouds in and around them. This black light we inhale through our nostrils in an effortless way. When it arrives at our heart, in an instant it becomes radiant clear light. As we exhale, this light streams back to all beings. It pervades them and gives each one great joy. We continue like this for as long as it feels right.

At the end, we wish that all the good which was now built up may benefit all beings.

Guru Yoga Meditation on the 16th Karmapa
(basic meditation of the Karma Kagyü Lineage)

This version of the Three-Light Meditation presented here, is taken from the Summer of 1995. Already in the late sixties, the 16th Karmapa, Rangjung Rigpe Dorje, made Hannah and myself holders of this practical and comprehensive tool for enlightenment, repeating his wish during later years that we always keep it fresh and on the cutting edge of the Western mind. For this reason, the focus of the practice has shifted several times. It is here directed towards actively continuing the pure view obtained during the meditation into one's daily life.

After having taken Refuge in the morning, one may informally and at any time during the day let the Lama appear in front of one and receive his blessing. I know of no more effective meditation. Therefore: *practice and enjoy.*

Guru Yoga Meditation

We feel the formless stream of air at the tip of our nose and let thoughts and feelings pass without evaluation. Then we focus on the four basic thoughts which turn mind towards liberation and enlightenment:

We recognize our precious opportunity in this life, that we can benefit countless beings through the methods of a Buddha. Few ever meet beyond-dualistic teachings and even fewer are able to use them.

We remember the impermanence of everything composite. Only the unlimited clear space of mind is lasting, and nobody knows how long conditions will remain for recognizing that.

We understand causality: that it is up to us what will come. Former thoughts, words and actions became our present state, and right now we are sowing the seeds of our future.

Finally we see the reasons for working with mind: enlightenment is timeless highest bliss, and we cannot benefit others while confused and suffering ourselves.

Not experiencing the world as we would wish to, we now open up to those who have that power. For the good of all beings we take Refuge in our goal, Buddha, the full development of mind; in the teachings (Dharma) which bring us there; in our friends and helpers (Sangha) on the way; and especially in the Lama, our teacher. In the Karma Kagyu lineage he always represents the Karmapa, at present the 17th Thaye Dorje in Delhi, India. Uniting blessing, methods, and protection, he is needed for our fast development.

Now out of space in front of us, condenses the golden, transparent form of the 16th Karmapa, the giver of this meditation. He is a radiant field of energy and light. He wears the Black Crown, the shape of which can awaken mind's deepest awareness, and his face is golden and mild. His eyes see us clearly; he knows us and wishes us everything good. Expressing the inseparable state of compassion and wisdom, of bliss and space, his crossed hands hold a dorje and bell at his heart. Seated in the Dorje-position, he is surrounded by masses of light.

We understand that he is no limited being but an expression of space as truth and the essence of all Buddhas. His presence is there whether we can see his form clearly or not, and we strongly desire to accomplish his qualities for the benefit of all. Knowing our wish, Karmapa comes ever closer, now remaining at a pleasant distance in front of us.

We think or say: "Dearest Lama, essence of all Buddhas, of you we ask: Give us your power which removes the ignorance and obscurations of all beings and ourselves. Let mind's timeless light awaken inside us."

*Responding to our strong wish, Karmapa smiles. Now a powerful clear light radiates from his forehead and enters the same place between our eyebrows. It fills our head with powerful crystalline light and dissolves all disturbing impressions in brain, nerves, and senses. The causes of harmful habits and diseases thus disappear, and our body becomes a conscious tool for bringing protection, love, and material things to others. While retaining the clear light for as long as desired, we hear the inner vibration of the syllable **OM**.*

*Now emanating from Karmapa's throat, a radiant beam of red light enters our mouth and throat. Transparent and powerful, it dissolves all difficulties in our speech. The impressions of negative confused words disappear, and our speech becomes compassion and wisdom, a conscious tool for benefiting others. Together with the red light, we hear the deep inner vibrations of the syllable **AH**.*

*Now from the heart-center in the middle of Karmapa's chest, an intense blue light shines out. It streams into the middle of our chest and fills it up. Thus mental difficulties disappear. Disturbing feelings and stiff ideas dissolve, and our mind becomes spontaneous joy, space, and bliss inseparable. Inseparable from the deep blue light vibrates the syllable **HUNG**.*

Then the three lights enter us at the same time. Clear light fills our head, red light our throat, and blue light our heart. We remain in this essential state, encompassing all, for as long as time permits.

The 16th Karmapa, Rangjung Rigpe Dorje (1924-1981)

While receiving the lights, we can use a mantra to further unite inner and outer truth, here in its expression as power.

Each repetition of the mantra, Karmapa Chenno: "Power of all the Buddhas, work through us, become one with us," puts us in the stream of enlightened activity. We repeat it loudly or inwardly for as long as we like while absorbing the lights.

Karmapa Chenno

(repeat mantra as long as you wish)

Then the golden form of Karmapa and his Black Crown dissolve into rainbow light. It flows through us, and all form disappears. Now there is only awareness with no middle or end, timeless and everywhere. Though thoughts or sensory impressions may appear, they are nothing but the free play of that space.

When this state can no longer be held, again a world manifests, perfect and pure. Every atom vibrates with joy and is kept together by love. All is fresh and meaningful, radiant with unlimited potential. Beings near and far appear as female or male Buddhas, whether they know it or not. Sounds are mantras and thoughts wisdom, for the sole reason that they can happen.

Also our own body now condenses out of space, appearing as our preferred Buddha, our Lama, or as our habitual form. But there is now one major difference from before the meditation. Then we were our body and thus vulnerable to old age, sickness and death. Now, instead, we have our body. Body and speech are our tools for benefiting others. What we really are— and we know that now—is that clear light which was conscious also when there was no form.

We decide to keep this pure view in all situations of life and strengthen it whenever possible. Finally we wish that the good which just appeared may become limitless, stream out to all beings everywhere, remove all their suffering, and bring them the only lasting joy, that of knowing their mind.

FINAL WORDS

So what awaits the hopefuls who—inspired by this book—call the addresses below and find a local Kagyu group?

First, a friendly, open reception, I hope, and an assortment of useful books. Then, if they want to work with themselves in a goal-oriented way, an assortment of power-tools lie ready. Practices for body, speech, and mind involving nearly countless repetitions will be presented, and through them, one's mind will experience its full athletic capacities for ups and downs. Gradually, however, and especially when not expected, a steadily growing joy will manifest, and finally one experiences meaning without end. To help my students anticipate what lies ahead, I sometimes explain the process like this:

At the outset of your development, your ego still thinks it is gaining ground. Its attitude is more or less as follows: "Before I was great, and now I have also become spiritual. I'm with the free Karma Kagyu, the happiest Yogis of all, and soon I shall know what my Lama knows." This state is pleasant but also sticky, and Buddha's timeless wisdom deliberately targets it. Joining a noble company is not for free, and though your ego may still enjoy the bread and potatoes of its habitual patterns for a while, if your Lama is skillful, that is all it gets. Each Buddhist group has a more or less effective ego-diet which expresses its teacher's powerfield, be it the renunciation of the Theravada, the discipline of Zen, or the full range of practical methods of the three "old" Tibetan schools.

With some, morality is important; with others, humility or learnedness; some make compassion or wisdom into the way. My students are instructed to show a stiff upper lip, to become fearless and joyful.

Thus cheated of its expected meat and salad through the lack of emotionality and dramas, your ego will become suspicious. It will sow doubts, complaints such as back pain, and sudden cravings for meaningless activity, all in order to protect itself.

At this point, the Bodhisattva vows will be presented as enticing junk food, and once again your strong but stupid illusions of a "self" will swallow the bait. The idea of being the one to save all beings will make one feel recognized and think: "At long last my true importance is being recognized." This only makes one walk further into the trap.

This is a major misjudgment because here the sufferings of the ego really start. Every thought of others draws energy from its own trips, and each realization of emptiness is pure ego-poison. Just as it wants to congratulate itself on having been especially good, instead of the expected gratification, another job comes up and, though it may compliment itself that it understands emptiness better than others, still the frequent teaching that neither your body nor mind contain any real or lasting essence or self will dig at its roots.

Already quite knocked out, your ego may try to muddle its way around the situation, and here your clearest warning signs are a tendency towards holy pretense and ceremony, combined with growing frustration. It is the revenge of a severely wounded self, and it often takes the perverse direction of trying to limit the freedom of others. Whether residual Christianity, unresolved defeats in your life, or a joyless understanding of ethics are its cause: if you see this happening, it's time to go to a Lama with humor and life-experience. Working with your totality, such a teacher can make you cross this hurdle and thus shift your inner development into next gear.

If at that stage your devotion or wish for freedom are not sufficient, or the Lama chosen is not able to take you through, some decide to progress gradually in a protected environment by taking monastic or other outer vows.

If you neither conquer life in its fullness, however, nor put yourself under some kind of guiding discipline, there exists the danger of getting stuck in a limbo. Basically dissatisfied, you must be very careful not to become a well-informed but sour senior member that your local Buddhist center would be delighted to get rid of!

Therefore, please always trust your understanding of mind's freedom. Rely on a Lama with both transmission and life experience, and feel at home in the finest company of the Diamond Way and the Mahamudra. Like a hundred Vikings storming a fort, your confidence in space as joy will conquer the last bastion of your ego. Now left with no other nourishment than the finding of faults with others, the recognition of each disturbing feeling as, in essence, enlightened wisdom, and all doubt as steps on one's way, will spontaneously free your mind's full potential. What was left of your ego will fall five yards into the ground, gradually disappear in smoke, and you will stay in boundless space and joy, your timeless state.

NOTES

[1]Refuge (Tib: Dhyab Dro) is the meeting with one's own Buddha nature. Through a short ritual, one aligns oneself with values on which one can truly rely. This means the Buddha-state as the goal, his teachings as the way, and one's friends as helpers along that way. In the Diamond Way, one also takes refuge in the Lama, the source of blessing, spiritual power and meaningful protection.

[2]Emptiness (Tib.: Tongpanyi / Skt: Shunyata) means that nothing arises by itself but is based on conditions. It describes the ultimate nature of all outer and inner phenomena and though it is realized in flashes of insight between thoughts, comprehending it through concepts is major brain-gymnastics.

[3]Mantra (Tib: Ngag): Natural vibration usually of the heart-center of a Buddha aspect. Should be spoken as transmitted by one's teacher. Wherever Mantras are used, enlightened energies condense. It is a main element of the Diamond Way.

[4]Center: place where people interested in Buddhism meet regularly for teachings and guided meditations.

[5]Empowerment (Tib.: Wang / Skt.: Abisheka) A ceremony by which the practicing student is introduced to the energy field of a certain Buddha aspect and receives the empowerment to meditate on this aspect.

[6]"Bum-lung" combines the two forms with the "tri" or the actual method of practice.

[7]Protectors: the most important protectors are direct emanations of the Buddhas: male Mahakalas and female Mahakalis. During Buddhist refuge they promise to turn every experience into a step on a student's way to enlightenment.

Buddhist Centers
of the Karma Kagyu Lineage
under the spiritual guidance of the 17th Karmapa
Thaye Dorje and directed by Lama Ole Nydahl

Main centers out of a total of 180.

USA

Buddhist Center Kamtsang Choling
San Francisco
(main center in the USA)
110 Merced Ave.,
San Francisco, CA 94127
Tel: 415-661-6467
Fax: 415-665-2241
E-mail:
74034.10331@compuserve.com

Buddhist Center Houston
c/o Torre Fossum
804 Tall Pines
Friendswood, TX 77046
Tel: 713-482-2926
Fax: 713-482-2606
E-mail:
102041.2162@compuserve.com

Buddhist Center Los Angeles
c/o Karin Grillitz
432 S. Curzon Ave. Apt. 2B
Los Angeles, CA 90036
Tel: 213-93111903
Fax: 213-931-0909

Buddhist Group Miami
c/o Nicole Rill
1649 Bay Dr.,
Miami Beach, FL 33141
Tel & Fax: 305-864-9914

Buddhist Group Nevada City
c/o Paul and Nancy Clemens
13386 N. Bloomfield Rd.
Nevada City, CA 95959
Tel: 916-265-5044
Fax: 916-265-0603

Buddhist Group New York
c/o Lisa and Tasso Kalianiotis
2372 36th St., Astoria, NY 11105
Tel: 718-278-7452
E-mail: tass@tribeca.ios.com

Buddhist Group Phoenix
c/o Joe Ciula
4128 N. 22nd St. #6
Phoenix, AZ 85016
Tel: 602-224-5864

Buddhist Group Albuquerque
c/o Kathleen Kess
1817 Don Felipe S.W.
Albuquerque, NM 87105
Tel: 505-873-2624
E-mail: kmkess@unm.edu

Buddhist Group San Diego
c/o Josh Russel
1507 Rubenstein
Solana Beach, CA 92075
Tel: 619-634-3972
E-mail: bbbrown@cts.com

Buddhist Center San Luis Obispo
c/o Nancy Reinstein
1745 Portola St.
San Louis Obispo, CA 93401
Tel: 805-541-8678
Fax: 805-544-7976

Buddhist Center Taos
c/o Norbert Ubechel
P.O. Box 696
El Prado, NM 87529
Tel: 505-758-4974

AUSTRALIA
Buddhist Group Perth
c/o Shona & Stewart Jarvis
unit 3 111 Stock Rd.
Attandale, WA 6156
Tel + Fax: 61-9-330 38 52

Buddhist Centre Sydney
c/o Donald Marshall
99 Gowrie Street
Newtown, NSW 2042
Tel: 61-2-419423939
Fax: 61-2-99694271

AUSTRIA
Buddhist Center Wien
Fleischmarkt 16
A-1010 Wien
Tel: 43-1-876 54 34
Fax: 43-1-876 54 34
E-mail: Reinhard.Belocky@
GBAT500.zamg.ac.at

CANADA
Buddhist Centre Edmonton
c/o Roy Beebe
11115-35A Avenue
Edmonton, Alberta T6J 0A4

Buddhist Group Vancouver
c/o Jolanta Pyra
#201-1230 E. 8th Ave.
Vancouver, BC V5T1V2
Tel: 604-876-3875
Fax: 604-875-9606

Buddhist Group Montreal
c/o Lara Braitstein
P.O. Box 385
Hudson Heights, J0P 1J0 Quebec
Tel: 514-458-4640

COLOMBIA
Buddhist Center Bogota
c/o Eduardo Velazquez
Calle 87 #11A-42, Bogota
Tel: 57-3-218 33 15
Fax: 57-1-337 99 31
Attn. Carlos Velazquez

DENMARK
Buddhist Center København
Svanemøllevej 56
DK-2100 København Ø
Tel: 45-39-29 27 11
Fax: 45-39-29 57 33
E-mail: kdl-cph@postl.tele.dk

GERMANY
Buddhist Center Hamburg
Stahltwiete 20
D-22761 Hamburg
Tel: 49-40-389 36 31
Fax: 49-40-389 87 02
E-mail:
100600.3234@compuserve.com

Buddhist Center Wuppertal
Heinkelstr. 27
D-42285 Wuppertal
Tel: 49-202-840 80 / 840 89
Fax: 49-202-828 45
E-mail:
100671.2041@compuserve.com

Haus Schwarzenberg
Hinterschwarzenberg 8
D-87466 Oy-Mittelberg
Tel: 49-8366-98380
Fax: 49-8366-983818
E-mail:
haus.schwarzenberg@t-online.de

GREAT BRITAIN
Buddhist Group Cambridge
c/o Matthew Huddleston
34 Pakenham Close
Cambridge CB4 1PW, UK
Tel: 44-402693821
Fax: 44-1223-312209
E-mail: mrh1005@cam.ac.uk

HUNGARY
Buddhist Center Budapest
c/o Istvan & Eva Gruber
Buday Laszlo u. 7, alag.1
H-1024 Budapest
Tel: 36-1-274 10 06
Fax: 36-1-274 10 06
E-mail:
100324.435@compuserve.com

NEW ZEALAND
Buddhist Center Christchurch
c/o Barbara & Manfred Ingerfeld
127 Knowles St.Christchurch 5
Tel: 64-3-3555 992
Fax: 64-3-3642 083
Attn. Manfred Ingerfeld

Buddhist Retreat Kaitaia
P.O. Box 444
RDI Kaitaia

PERU
Buddhist Center Lima
c/o Ricardo La Serna
Gral. Mendiburu 842
Miraflores-Lima 18
Tel: 51-14-413 652
Fax: 51-14-413 652

POLAND
Buddhist Center Warszawa
c/o Mira Boboli
Anielewicza 4/79
PL-00-157 Warszawa
Tel: 48-22-31 14 73
Fax: 48-22-46 02 78
E-Mail: glus@bevy.hsn.com.pl
Attn. Mira Boboli

Buddhist Retreat Kuchary
Kuchary 57
PL-09-210 Drobin
Tel: 48-24-75 68 20
Fax: 48-24-62 87 21
Tel & Fax: Buddhist Center

RUSSIA
Buddhist Center Petersburg
c/o Sasha Koibagarov
ul. Varshavskaya 16 - 17
196 105 St. Petersburg
Tel: 7-812-142-9883
Fax: 7-812-142-9883
E-mail: grisha@kll.spb.su

SPAIN
Buddhist Retreat Karma Gon
Atalaya Alta
Apartado 179
E-29700 Velez-Malaga
Tel: 34-5-211-5197
Fax: 34-5-211-5197
E-mail:
100517.1023@compuserve.com

SWITZERLAND
Buddhist Center Zürich
Hammerstr. 9a
CH-8008 Zürich
Tel: 41-1-382-0875
Fax: 41-1-380-0144
E-Mail:
100553.3425@compuserve.com

VENEZUELA
Buddhist Center Caracas
c/o Iris Hoogesteijn
Apto. 50731
Caracas 1050-A
Tel: 58-2-740 114
Fax: 58-2-513 381

ABOUT THE AUTHOR

Lama Ole Nydahl was born in Denmark in 1941 to a loving family of professors and authors. During childhood he had frequent memories from his last life, battling Chinese soldiers to protect the civilians of eastern Tibet, and neither his wildness nor idealism suffered in his transition to the West. While growing up he gained quite a reputation as a nearly undefeated boxer and unflinching protector of his friends.

After military service, he completed a philosophical degree at the University of Copenhagen and studied English and German in different countries. He started a doctorate on the gratifying vision of Aldous Huxley and soon became a leading European exponent of the culture of the sixties.

In 1968, on a honeymoon to Nepal with his childhood love, Hannah, their vocation became clear. Recognized as former protectors and Lamas of the Karma Kagyu Lineage by the 16th Karmapa, Tibet's first incarnate Lama, they meditated for three years in the eastern Himalayas. Then he sent them home to prepare for his arrival and to teach.

Entering the Diamond Way (256 pages, $14.95) is Lama Ole's account of the years until their return. It is a very uplifting book. As they were still consumers of Buddhism at that time, they could permit themselves to focus on the positive aspects.

Riding the Tiger (512 pages, $17.95), a further autobiographical novel, covers twenty years of constant growth from the autumn of 1972 and includes over 350 photos of places and people met on their travels. Written from a position of responsibility, this book employs a long-range and critical viewpoint, and, as Danes don't respect holy cows, politically correct people often cringe at Lama Ole's candid and sweeping statements. There exists, however, no more informative book on the development of living Western Buddhism, and sharing in so much human growth is breathtaking.

Hannah, Lama Ole, and recently Caty and Tomek—known collectively as TCHO—have so far started 180 centers worldwide for the Karma Kagyu lineage. Hannah increasingly assists Kunzig Shamarpa, the senior lineage-holder of the school. Each center has leaders, and Lama Ole has asked several of his students to travel and teach. It is his deepest wish to make the skillful methods of the Diamond Way relevant to the independent and educated West.

During the early nineties, their organization stopped the world's acceptance of a fake communist Chinese candidate for the new Karmapa, and in 1994 they were instrumental in getting the 17th Karmapa, Thaye Dorje, to freedom in India, where he now resides.

In spite of yearly visits to nearly all the centers and teaching courses to thousands of people, Lama Ole has managed also to write a half dozen books on central Buddhist topics, which are translated into nearly a score of languages. There are also eight meditation booklets, videos, and audios. All the English books are published by Blue Dolphin Publishing, Nevada City, California. They have not been edited into sweet nothings chasing the spirit of the time, and sales grow by the year.

Entering the Diamond Way
My Path Among the Lamas

The adventure begins as Ole and Hannah set out on their honeymoon to Nepal in the late '60s. Their first contact with Tibetan Buddhism in Kathmandu—a lama who disappears right before their eyes—led to their training with some of the highest lamas of the Kagyu lineage.

ISBN: 0-931892-03-1, 256 pp., 16 full color & 60 b/w photos, paper, $14.95

"One cannot really transmit anything, except what one has directly experienced, and the reason many of you will be able to identify with what happened to us is that, deep within, we are so very much alike." —Lama Ole Nydahl

Riding the Tiger
Twenty Years on the Road: The Risks and Joys of Bringing Tibetan Buddhism to the West

The story continues as Ole and Hannah introduce Tibetan Buddhism and establish over 100 centers all over the world, with many intriguing cross-cultural adventures and teachings along the way—from the spiritually hungry of Russia to bandits in South America and travels in N. America with Karmapa and Kalu Rinpoche.

ISBN: 0-931892-67-8, 512 pp., 380 photos, paper, $17.95

Practical Buddhism
The Kagyu Path
Lama Ole Nydahl & Carol Aronoff
ISBN: 0-931892-63-5, 48 pp., paper, $5.00

Ngöndro
The Four Foundational Practices of Tibetan Buddhism
Lama Ole Nydahl
ISBN: 0-931892-23-6, 96 pp., paper, $9.95

Teachings on the Nature of Mind
Lama Ole Nydahl
ISBN: 0-931892-58-9, 40 pp., paper, $5.00

Mahamudra
Boundless Joy and Freedom
Lama Ole Nydahl
ISBN: 0-931892-69-4, 96 pp., paper, $9.95